Soufflé Recipes

A Simply Savory Cookbook with Delicious Soufflé Recipes

By
BookSumo Press
All rights reserved

Published by
http://www.booksumo.com

ENJOY THE RECIPES?

KEEP ON COOKING WITH 6 MORE FREE COOKBOOKS!

Visit our website and simply enter your email address to join the club and receive your 6 cookbooks.

http://booksumo.com/magnet

https://www.instagram.com/booksumopress/

https://www.facebook.com/booksumo/

LEGAL NOTES

All Rights Reserved. No Part Of This Book May Be Reproduced Or Transmitted In Any Form Or By Any Means. Photocopying, Posting Online, And / Or Digital Copying Is Strictly Prohibited Unless Written Permission Is Granted By The Book's Publishing Company. Limited Use Of The Book's Text Is Permitted For Use In Reviews Written For The Public.

Table of Contents

Creamy Sour Corn Soufflé 9

Easter Soufflé 10

November's Soufflé 11

Flapjack Soufflé 12

Nebraska Fish Soufflé 13

German Soufflé 14

Sweet French Bread Soufflé 15

American Gratin Soufflé 16

Bittersweet Soufflé 17

Soufflé Mornings 18

Cottage Broccoli Soufflé 19

Parsley and Mushroom Soufflé 20

Latin Parmesan Soufflé 21

Rolled Oat Soufflé 22

Mesa Breakfast Soufflé 23

Monterey Soufflé 24

North African Chickpea Sandwich 25

Cream Cheese Soufflé Dip 26

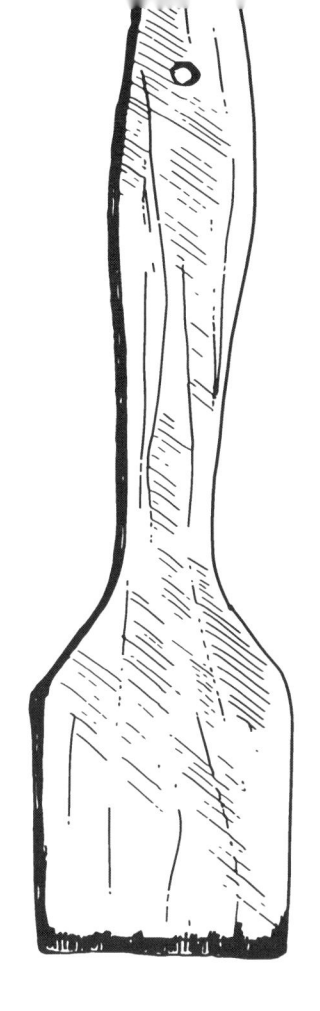

Savory Leafy Green Soufflé 27

Mediterranean Soufflé 28

Cheddar Squash Soufflé 30

Citrus Pastry Soufflé 31

Tomato & Chives Soufflé 32

Carolina Grits Soufflé 33

Crab & Egg Soufflé 34

Minced Rice Soufflé 35

Ketogenic Soufflé 36

Soufflé Bites 37

Swiss Chocolate Soufflé 38

Chinese Soufflé 40

Goat Cheese and Chives Soufflé 41

5-Ingredient Soufflé 42

Southwest Soufflé 43

Cauliflower Soufflé 44

Watercress Lemon Soufflé 45

Hot Corn Soufflé 47

Spicer Spinach Soufflé 48

Leftover Soufflé 49

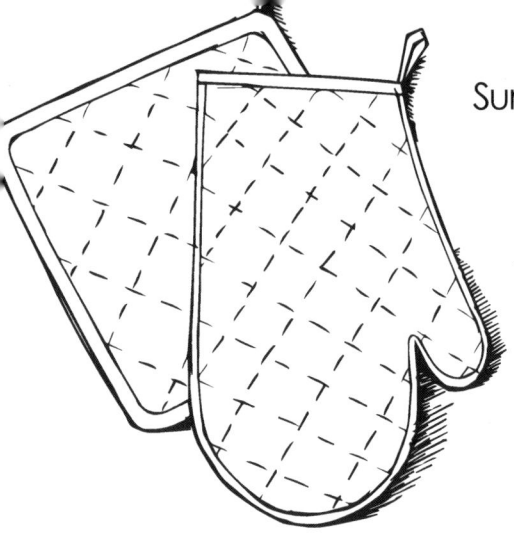

Sun-Dried Tomato Soufflé 50

Milky White Soufflé 52

Soufflé in its Simplest 54

Maple Soufflé 55

Chipotle Soufflé 56

Big Apple Soufflé 57

Western European Soufflé 58

How to Make a Soufflé 59

Brazilian Fruit Soufflé 60

Mint Cocoa Soufflé 61

Sweet Ricotta Soufflé 62

Dry Mustard Soufflé 63

Spicy Bell Mushroom Soufflé 64

Buttery Challah Soufflé 65

August Berry Soufflé 66

Green Onion Swiss Shrimp Soufflé 67

Idaho Potato Soufflé 69

Thai Curry Soufflé 70

Pecan Soufflé 71

Honey Butter Soufflé 72

Alternative Leek Soufflé 73

5-Ingredient Corn Soufflé 74

Pistachios Soufflé 75

Caster Espresso Soufflé 77

Lemony Applesauce Soufflé 78

Matzo American Soufflé 79

4-Ingredient Soufflé 80

Deep Vanilla Soufflé 81

2-Cheese Fruity Soufflé 83

Denver Soufflé 85

2-Pineapple Soufflé 86

Authentic Vegan Soufflé 87

Burrito Soufflé 88

Chicken & Mushroom Soufflé 89

Scallion Soufflé 90

Lemon Soufflé 91

Noodles & Spinach Soufflé 92

Cheese & Bread Soufflé 93

Phyllo Cups Soufflé 94

Cheddar Soufflé 96

Spiced Soufflé 97

Tangerine Soufflé 98

Sausage Soufflé 99

Crab & Coconut Soufflé 100

Cheesy Herb Soufflé 101

Potato Soufflé 102

Mac & Cheese Soufflé 103

Lemony Raspberry Soufflé 104

Pepperoni & Cheese Soufflé 105

Milky Asparagus Soufflé 106

Pumpkin Soufflé 107

Nutty Pecan Soufflé 108

Carrot Soufflé 109

Squash & Applesauce Soufflé 110

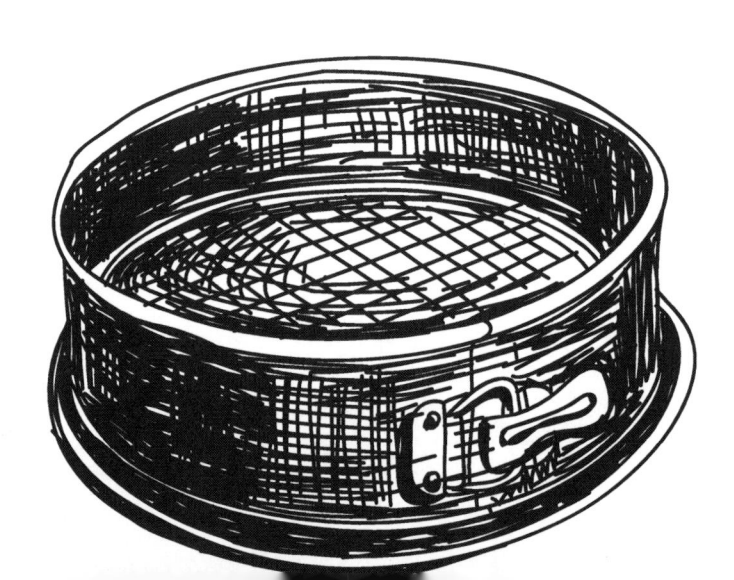

Creamy Sour Corn Soufflé

🥣 Prep Time: 10 mins
🕒 Total Time: 45 mins

Servings per Recipe: 4
Calories   235.1
Fat   10.0g
Cholesterol   122.6mg
Sodium   517.3mg
Carbohydrates   32.3g
Protein   6.9g

Ingredients

- 2 eggs
- 2 tbsp cornstarch
- 2 tbsp sugar
- 1/4 tsp salt
- 1/8 tsp pepper
- 1 dash nutmeg
- 1 (14-16 oz.) cans creamed corn
- 1/2 C. sour cream
- 1/2 C. milk

Directions

1. Set your oven to 400 degrees F before doing anything else and arrange a rack in the center of oven. Grease an 8-inch square baking dish.
2. In a bowl, crack the eggs and with an electric mixer, beat until foamy.
3. Add the remaining ingredients and beat until well combined.
4. Place the mixture into prepared baking dish.
5. Cook in the oven for about 35 minutes or till a toothpick inserted in the center comes out clean.

EASTER
Soufflé

🥣 Prep Time: 1 hr
🕐 Total Time: 1 hr 10 mins

Servings per Recipe: 6
Calories	433.7
Fat	18.0g
Cholesterol	133.6mg
Sodium	340.3mg
Carbohydrates	65.6g
Protein	4.9g

Ingredients

1 1/2 lb. carrots, sliced
1/2 C. butter
3 eggs
1 tsp vanilla
1/4 C. all-purpose flour

1 1/2 tsp baking powder
1 1/2 C. sugar
3/4 tsp ground cinnamon

Directions

1. Set your oven to 350 degrees F before doing anything else and lightly, grease 1 1/2-quart soufflé dish.
2. In a pan of water, add carrots and bring to a boil.
3. Cook for about 20-25 minutes. Drain well.
4. In a food processor, add the coked carrots and remaining ingredients and pulse
5. until smooth.
6. Transfer the mixture into the prepared soufflé dish evenly.
7. Cook in the oven for about 1 hour and 10 minutes..

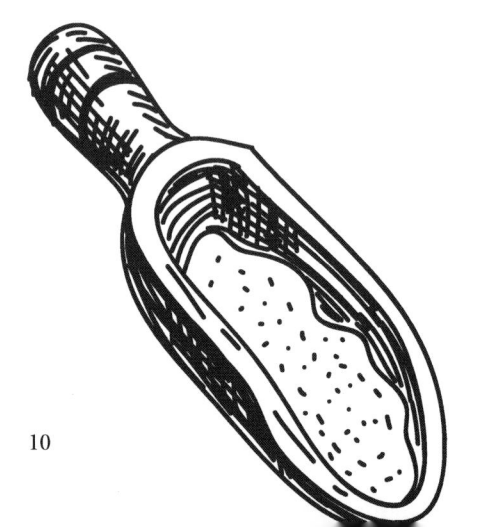

November's Soufflé

🥣 Prep Time: 10 mins
🕐 Total Time: 45 mins

Servings per Recipe: 8
Calories 429.8
Fat 19.3g
Cholesterol 75.3mg
Sodium 263.2mg
Carbohydrates 62.2g
Protein 4.7g

Ingredients

3 C. sweet potatoes, mashed (canned)
3/4 C. sugar
1/2 tsp salt
2 eggs
1/4 C. butter
1/2 C. milk
1 tsp vanilla

Garnish
1 C. brown sugar
1 C. chopped pecans
1/3 C. flour
1/4 C. butter, melted

Directions

1. Set your oven to 350 degrees F before doing anything else and grease a 9x2-inch round baking dish.
2. In a bowl, add the sweet potatoes, sugar, salt, eggs 1/4 C. of the butter, milk and vanilla and mix until well combined.
3. For topping: in another bowl, add all ingredients and mix well.
4. Place the sweet potato mixture into the prepared baking dish evenly and sprinkle with topping mixture.
5. Cook in the oven for about 35 minutes.

FLAPJACK
Soufflé

🥣 Prep Time: 10 mins
🕐 Total Time: 30 mins

Servings per Recipe: 8
Calories   243.4
Fat   16.0g
Cholesterol   152.0mg
Sodium   164.7mg
Carbohydrates   16.9g
Protein   7.3g

Ingredients

1/2 C. butter
5 eggs
1 1/4 C. milk

1 1/4 C. all-purpose flour
1 tsp vanilla

Directions

1. Set your oven to 425 degrees F before doing anything else.
2. In the bottom of 9X13-inch baking dish, add the butter and place in the oven to melt, while preheating.
3. In a blender, add eggs and pulse until beaten.
4. Add the milk, flour and vanilla extract and pulse for about 30 seconds.
5. Place the mixture into the baking dish with melted butter.
6. Cook in the oven for about 20 minutes.

Nebraska
Fish Soufflé

🥣 Prep Time: 15 mins
🕐 Total Time: 40 mins

Servings per Recipe: 4
Calories   244.3
Fat   16.3g
Cholesterol   190.4mg
Sodium   772.5mg
Carbohydrates   7.5g
Protein   16.1g

Ingredients

3 tbsp butter
3 tbsp flour
1 C. milk
1 tsp salt
pepper (to taste)

1 (6 oz.) cans salmon, flaked and bones crushed
3 eggs, separated

Directions

1. Set your oven to 350 degrees F before doing anything else and grease a soufflé dish.
2. In a small pan, melt the butter and stir in the milk, flour, salt and pepper until well combined.
3. Cook until the mixture becomes thick.
4. Meanwhile, in a small bowl, add the egg yolks and beat slightly.
5. Remove from heat and stir in the salmon and egg yolks.
6. In a small bowl, add the egg whites and beat until stiff peaks form.
7. Place the mixture into the prepared soufflé dish evenly.
8. Cook in the oven for about 20 - 25 minutes.

GERMAN
Soufflé

🥣 Prep Time: 20 mins
🕐 Total Time: 35 mins

Servings per Recipe: 2
Calories   674.6
Fat   57.9g
Cholesterol   214.0mg
Sodium   122.8mg
Carbohydrates   51.3g
Protein   17.6g

Ingredients

1 oz. heavy cream
4 oz. dark chocolate
1/2 tbsp butter
2 large eggs (separated into whites and yolks)
1 dash cream of tartar
1/4 C. sugar

Topping:
berries
2 pieces dark chocolate
powdered sugar

Directions

1. Set your oven to 375 degrees F before doing anything else and arrange rack in the middle of oven.
2. Grease 2 (6-oz.) ramekins with some cold butter and then, dust with some granulated sugar and cocoa powder. Shake and roll each ramekin to coat the bottom and sides evenly.
3. In the double boiler, add the cream, butter and chocolate and melt, stirring frequently.
4. Remove from the heat. Add the two egg yolks into the chocolate mixture and beat until well combined.
5. In a bowl, add the egg whites and cream of tartar and beat until soft peaks are formed.
6. Add the sugar and beat until stiff peaks are formed. Slowly and gently, fold whipped egg whites into the chocolate mixture.
7. Divide the mixture into the prepared ramekins about 3/4 of the way up.
8. Place a piece of chocolate or berries on top of each ramekin and gently, push into the mixture. Arrange the ramekins into a baking dish and cook in the oven for about 15 minutes. Remove from the oven and dust with the sugar.
9. Serve immediately with a garnishing of the berries.

Sweet French Bread Soufflé

Prep Time: 10 mins
Total Time: 1 hr 5 mins

Servings per Recipe: 12
Calories   811.5
Fat   29.0g
Cholesterol   249.5mg
Sodium   1101.2mg
Carbohydrates   108.9g
Protein   29.3g

Ingredients

- 1/2 C. butter, softened
- 8 oz. cream cheese
- 1/2 C. maple syrup
- 2 loaves French bread, cubed
- 12 eggs
- 3 C. half-and-half
- 1 1/2 tsp vanilla
- ground cinnamon, for dusting
- powdered sugar, for dusting

Directions

1. Grease 2 (7x11-inch) baking dishes with some butter.
2. Place bread cubes into prepared baking dishes about half way full.
3. In a small bowl, add the cream cheese, butter and maple syrup and mix until well combined.
4. In another large bowl, add the half-and-half, eggs and vanilla and beat until well combined.
5. Place the cream cheese mixture over bread cubes evenly, followed by the egg mixture.
6. Sprinkle with the cinnamon and refrigerate, covered overnight.
7. Set your oven to 350 degrees F.
8. Remove the baking dish from refrigerator and cook in the oven for about 55-60 minutes.
9. Remove from the oven and serve with a dusting of the powdered sugar.

AMERICAN
Gratin Soufflé

🥣 Prep Time: 25 mins
🕐 Total Time: 55 mins

Servings per Recipe: 4
Calories   297.7
Fat   18.5g
Cholesterol   127.7mg
Sodium   351.1mg
Carbohydrates   26.1g
Protein   8.2g

Ingredients

1 large eggplant, pared and cubed
2 beaten eggs
1/2 C. milk
1/2 C. dry breadcrumbs
1 C. shredded American cheese
1/4 C. melted butter
3/4 C. crushed crackers

Directions

1. Set your oven to 350 degrees F before doing anything else and grease a casserole dish.
2. In a pan of salted boiling water, cook the eggplant cubes for about 15 minutes.
3. Drain the eggplant cubes well and transfer into a a bowl.
4. With a fork, mash the eggplant cubes well.
5. Add the 3/4 C. of the cheese, milk, eggs, breadcrumbs, salt and pepper and mix until well combined.
6. In another small bowl, add the crackers and melted butter and mix well.
7. Place the eggplant mixture into the prepared casserole dish evenly and top with the cracker mixture, followed by the remaining 1/4 C. of the cheese.
8. Cook in the oven for about 30 minutes.

Bittersweet Soufflé

🥣 Prep Time: 15 mins
🕐 Total Time: 27 mins

Servings per Recipe: 12
Calories   216.4
Fat   17.7g
Cholesterol   133.6mg
Sodium   170.6mg
Carbohydrates   11.4g
Protein   3.5g

Ingredients

- 8 oz. bittersweet chocolate, chopped
- 8 oz. butter, diced
- 6 eggs
- 4 oz. sugar
- 1 oz. sifted flour
- nonstick cooking spray

Directions

1. Set your oven to 325 degrees F before doing anything else and grease 12 soufflé dishes with non-stick spray.
2. In the top of a double boiler, place the chocolate and butter and heat until melted, stirring continuously.
3. In a bowl, add the eggs and sugar and beat until light and fluffy.
4. Add the flour into the bowl of chocolate mixture and mix well
5. Gently fold the chocolate mixture into the flour mixture.
6. Place the mixture into the prepared soufflé dishes evenly.
7. Cook in the oven for about 9-12 minutes.
8. Serve immediately.

SOUFFLÉ
Mornings

🥣 Prep Time: 10 mins
🕐 Total Time: 55 mins

Servings per Recipe: 6
Calories 445.3
Fat 29.2g
Cholesterol 297.9mg
Sodium 1168.3mg
Carbohydrates 17.2g
Protein 27.0g

Ingredients

1 lb. mild bulk beef sausage
6 eggs
2 C. milk
1 tsp salt
1 tsp dry mustard

6 slices white bread (cubed)
1 C. cheddar cheese (grated)

Directions

1. Heat a skillet and cook the crumbled sausage until browned.
2. Drain the grease and keep aside to cool.
3. In a large bowl, add the eggs, add milk, dry mustard and salt and beat well.
4. Add the bread cubes and stir to combine.
5. Add the cheese and browned sausage and mix well.
6. Refrigerate, covered overnight.
7. Set your oven to 350 degrees F.
8. Cook in the oven for about 45 minutes.

Cottage Broccoli Soufflé

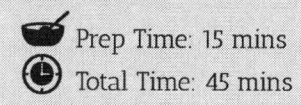

Prep Time: 15 mins
Total Time: 45 mins

Servings per Recipe: 4
Calories   431.6
Fat   33.3g
Cholesterol   189.9mg
Sodium   777.6mg
Carbohydrates   12.7g
Protein   21.8g

Ingredients

- 4 C. fresh broccoli, cut into small florets
- 2 tbsp water
- 5 tbsp margarine, melted
- 2 tbsp flour
- 3 eggs, beaten
- 1 C. small curd cottage cheese, drained
- 1/2 C. half-and-half cream
- 1 C. shredded cheddar cheese, divided
- 1/2 C. minced onion
- 1/4 tsp salt
- 1/2 tsp seasoning salt
- 1/2 tsp white pepper

Directions

1. Set your oven to 350 degrees F before doing anything else and grease a 7x11-inch baking dish.
2. In a microwave-safe bowl, add the cauliflower and water and microwave on High for about 3 minutes.
3. Remove from the microwave and stir in the margarine.
4. Then, sprinkle with the flour and toss to coat well.
5. In a large bowl, add the eggs, cream, cottage cheese, 1/2 C. of the cheese, onion, seasoned salt, salt nd white pepper and mix until well combined.
6. Add the broccoli and estir to combine.
7. Transfer the mixture into the prepared baking dish and top wit the 1/2 C. of cheese evenly.
8. Cook in the oven for about 30-35.

PARSLEY and Mushroom Soufflé

🥣 Prep Time: 10 mins
🕐 Total Time: 20 mins

Servings per Recipe: 4
Calories   198.2
Fat   16.6g
Cholesterol   250.7mg
Sodium   190.7mg
Carbohydrates   2.0g
Protein   10.0g

Ingredients

4 large eggs, separated
1 pinch salt and pepper
2 tsp fresh parsley, chopped
4 tbsp cream
1 tbsp butter

4 tbsp Brie cheese, roughly chopped
1/4 C. sautéed mushroom
1/4 C. sautéed onion

Directions

1. Set your oven to 350 degrees F before doing anything else.
2. In a bowl, add the egg yolks and beat until thick and light in color.
3. Add the cream, parsley, salt and pepper and stir to combine.
4. In another bowl, add the egg whites and beat until peaks form.
5. Gently, fold the whites into the yolk mixture.
6. Add the mushrooms and onions and gently, toss to coat well.
7. In a cast iron pan, melt the butter and cook the omelet mixture until firm on the bottom.
8. Transfer the pan into the oven and cook for about 3 minutes.
9. Now, sprinkle with the cheese and cook for about 2 minutes further.
10. Remove from the oven and fold the omelet in half before serving.

Latin Parmesan Soufflé

Prep Time: 30 mins
Total Time: 1 hr 15 mins

Servings per Recipe: 8
Calories	367.7
Fat	20.3g
Cholesterol	135.4mg
Sodium	1261.0mg
Carbohydrates	18.5g
Protein	27.3g

Ingredients

- 2 tbsp butter
- 5 medium Vidalia onions, chopped
- 2 C. fresh bread cubes (crusts removed)
- 1 (12 oz.) cans fat-free evaporated milk
- 3 large eggs
- 1 (15 oz.) can shredded Parmesan cheese
- 1 tsp salt

Directions

1. Set your oven to 350 degrees F before doing anything else and lightly, grease a 1 1/2-quart soufflé dish.
2. In a large skillet, melt the butter over medium heat and cook the onions for about 10-15 minutes.
3. Transfer the onions into a large bowl.
4. Add the bread cubes, milk, eggs, 1 C. of the cheese and salt and gently, stir to combine.
5. Place the mixture into prepared soufflé dish and sprinkle with remaining 1/4 C. of the cheese.
6. Cook in the oven for about 25 minutes.

ROLLED OAT
Soufflé

🥣 Prep Time: 15 mins
🕒 Total Time: 50 mins

Servings per Recipe: 4
Calories 297.5
Fat 5.5g
Cholesterol 56.8mg
Sodium 268.8mg
Carbohydrates 54.9g
Protein 8.6g

Ingredients

1 C. skim milk
1 tbsp butter
3/4 C. quick-cooking rolled oats
1/3 C. sugar
1/4 tsp salt
1/2 tsp cinnamon
1/4 C. nonfat sour cream

1 egg, separated
1/3 C. dried sweetened cranberries
2 egg whites
1/4 C. firmly packed brown sugar

Directions

1. Set your oven to 400 degrees F before doing anything else and grease 4 (5-oz) Soufflé molds. Arrange the mols into a baking dish.
2. In a small pan, add the milk and butter and just bring to a boil.
3. Slowly, add the oats, stirring continuously.
4. Reduce the heat to medium-low and cook for about 1-2 minutes, stirring occasionally.
5. Remove from the heat and transfer the oat mixture into a large bowl.
6. Add sugar, 1 egg yolk, sour cream, cinnamon and and salt and stir until smooth.
7. Stir in the dried fruit and keep aside.
8. In another bowl, add 3 egg whites and beat until stiff but not dry.
9. Gently fold the whipped egg whites into oat mixture.
10. Divide the mixture into the prepared molds evenly and sprinkle with the brown sugar.
11. Cook in the oven for about 15-20 minutes.
12. Serve immediately.

Mesa Breakfast Soufflé

🍳 Prep Time: 30 mins
🕐 Total Time: 1 hr 15 mins

Servings per Recipe: 6
Calories   334.3
Fat   19.4g
Cholesterol   175.5mg
Sodium   694.1mg
Carbohydrates   23.5g
Protein   15.9g

Ingredients

- 1 C. uncooked grits
- 4 C. boiling water
- 1 tsp salt
- 2 C. shredded sharp cheddar cheese
- 1/2 C. chopped onion
- 1 garlic clove, crushed
- 2 tbsp melted butter
- 1/3 C. finely chopped jalapeño pepper
- 4 egg yolks
- 4 egg whites

Directions

1. Set your oven to 350 degrees F before doing anything else and grease a 2-quart casserole dish.
2. In a pan, mix the grits and salt into boiling water.
3. Cook for about 10-20 minutes, stirring frequently.
4. Add the cheese and stir until melted.
5. Meanwhile, in a skillet, melt the butter and sauté the onion and garlic until tender.
6. Transfer the onion mixture into the pan of grits with the jalapeño pepper and stir to combine.
7. In a bowl, add the egg yolks and beat slightly.
8. Add a small amount of hot grits into the bowl of the egg yolks and stir to combine well.
9. Add the egg yolk mixture into grits and mix well.
10. In a bowl, add the egg whites and beat until stiff.
11. Fold the egg whites into the grits.
12. Place the mixture into the prepared casserole dish.
13. Cook in the oven for about 45-50 minutes.

MONTEREY
Soufflé

Prep Time: 10 mins
Total Time: 1 hr 10 mins

Servings per Recipe: 8
Calories 344.8
Fat 24.4g
Cholesterol 294.0mg
Sodium 723.9mg
Carbohydrates 5.0g
Protein 26.0g

Ingredients

- 1 lb. Monterey Jack cheese, cubed
- 1 C. small curd cottage cheese
- 1 C. salsa
- 9 eggs
- 1 C. buttermilk

Directions

1. Set your oven to 425 degrees F before doing anything else and grease a 13x9-inch baking dish.
2. In the bottom of the prepared baking dish, arrange the layers of the Monterey Jack cheese, cottage cheese and salsa evenly.
3. In a bowl, add the buttermilk and eggs and beat until well combined.
4. Place the egg mixture over the cheese mixture evenly.
5. Cook in the oven for about 1 hour.
6. Remove from the oven and keep aside for about 5 minutes before serving.

North African Chickpea Sandwich

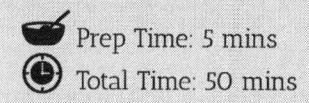

Prep Time: 5 mins
Total Time: 50 mins

Servings per Recipe: 8
Calories	292.2
Fat	16.4g
Cholesterol	23.2mg
Sodium	733.5mg
Carbohydrates	27.4g
Protein	8.9g

Ingredients

For Soufflé
- 2 C. chickpea flour
- 4 C. water
- 1/2 C. sunflower oil
- 2 -3 tsp salt
- 1/4 tsp black pepper
- 1 egg, beaten
- 1 1/2-2 tsp cumin

TO SERVE
- 4 tbsp harissa
- 2 large French baguettes
- 1 tbsp cumin

Directions

1. Set your oven to 350 degrees F before doing anything else.
2. For soufflé: in a large blender, add all the ingredients except egg and pulse until frothy and smooth.
3. Spread the beaten egg over the flour mixture evenly.
4. Transfer the mixture into a 7x11-inch rectangular Pyrex dish.
5. Cook in the oven for about 45 minutes.
6. With a cake knife, cut the soufflé into 8 pieces.
7. Cut each baguette into 1/4-inch slices and then split open.
8. Carefully, remove a little of the inner bread.
9. Spread about 1/2 tbsp of the harissa onto the bottom of each 1/4 of baguette and top each with a soufflé piece.
10. Sprinkle each piece with cumin and cover with the top of the baguette.
11. Serve Immediately.

CREAM CHEESE
Soufflé Dip

Prep Time: 5 mins
Total Time: 30 mins

Servings per Recipe: 6
Calories   630.5
Fat   55.0g
Cholesterol   159.3mg
Sodium   1022.6mg
Carbohydrates   15.8g
Protein   20.3g

Ingredients

3 (8 oz.) packages cream cheese, softened
2 C. Parmesan cheese
1/2 C. mayonnaise

1 (16 oz.) packages frozen chopped onions

Directions

1. Set your oven to 350 degrees F before doing anything else.
2. In the bottom of a 1-quart casserole dish, add all the ingredients and mix until well combined.
3. Cook in the oven for about 20-25 minutes.
4. Serve warm.

Savory Leafy Green Soufflé

Prep Time: 15 mins
Total Time: 1 hr 15 mins

Servings per Recipe: 6
Calories   148.2
Fat   4.4g
Cholesterol   144.8mg
Sodium   513.8mg
Carbohydrates   19.2g
Protein   9.3g

Ingredients

- 3 large onions, sliced thinly
- 2 oz. non-fat cooking spray
- 1 C. fat free sour cream
- 4 large eggs
- 10 oz. frozen spinach, thawed (water squeezed out)
- 1 tbsp horseradish
- 1 tsp salt
- 1 tsp pepper
- 2 tbsp flour
- 1 tsp caraway seed

Directions

1. Set your oven to 350 degrees F before doing anything else and grease a 1 1/2-quart casserole dish generously.
2. Grease a skillet with the cooking spray and heat it.
3. Add onions and sauté until golden.
4. Remove from the heat and keep aside to cool slightly.
5. In a blender, add the eggs and sour cream and pulse until well combined.
6. Transfer the egg mixture into a bowl with remaining ingredients and stir to combine well.
7. Place the mixture into the prepared casserole dish evenly.
8. Cook in the oven for about 45-60 minutes.

MEDITERRANEAN
Soufflé

Prep Time: 25 mins
Total Time: 57 mins

Servings per Recipe: 8
Calories   251.8
Fat   15.2g
Cholesterol   94.3mg
Sodium   335.6mg
Carbohydrates   14.3g
Protein   13.9g

Ingredients

3 tbsp butter
butter, for coating ramekins
1 C. dry breadcrumbs
3 tbsp cake flour
1 C. milk
10 oz. soft fresh goat cheese

3 egg yolks
salt and pepper
1 C. egg white

Directions

1. Set your oven to 425 degrees F before doing anything else and arrange a rack in the middle of the oven.
2. Grease 8 (5-oz.) ramekins with the butter generously and coat with the breadcrumbs evenly, shaking off the excess and reserving them.
3. In a stainless-steel skillet, melt 3 tbsp of the butter over medium-high heat.
4. Stir in the flour and cook for about 20 seconds, beating continuously.
5. Stir in the milk and cook for about 1 minute, beating continuously.
6. In a large bowl, add 8 oz. of the cheese and crumble it.
7. Add the hot milk mixture and mix well. Add the egg yolks, salt and pepper and mix until well combined.
8. In another large bowl, add the egg whites and with an electric mixer, with clean, dry beaters, beat until stiff peaks form. Fold half of the whipped egg whites into the cheese mixture. Gently, fold in the remaining whipped egg whites.
9. Divide half of the soufflé mixture into prepared ramekins evenly and top with the remaining 2 oz. of crumbled goat cheese.
10. Place the remaining half of the Soufflé mixture on top of each ramekin evenly and sprinkle with the reserved breadcrumbs.

11. Arrange the ramekins in a large baking dish and add enough boiling water to come halfway up the sides of the ramekins.
12. Cook in the oven for about 25 minutes.
13. Remove from the oven and keep in the water bath for about 15 minutes.
14. Carefully, run a knife around the edge of each soufflé and invert onto a baking sheet.
15. Keep aside at room temperature for up to 6 hours.
16. Set you oven to 425 degrees F and arrange a rack in the middle of the oven.
17. Cook in the oven for about 5-7 minutes.

CHEDDAR
Squash Soufflé

🥣 Prep Time: 15 mins
🕐 Total Time: 1 hr 15 mins

Servings per Recipe: 4
Calories   796.3
Fat   54.4g
Cholesterol   206.9mg
Sodium   1665.3mg
Carbohydrates   52.1g
Protein   26.3g

Ingredients

2 lb. yellow squash, sliced
1 medium onion, sliced
1 tsp salt
1/2 tsp sugar
6 tbsp butter, melted
3 tbsp flour

2 eggs, slightly beaten
1 C. milk
1/2 lb. sharp cheddar cheese, grated
1/2 box crackers, crumbled

Directions

1. Set your oven to 350 degrees F before doing anything else and grease a 1 1/2-quart casserole dish.
2. In a pan, add the squash, sugar, salt, black pepper and enough water to cover and simmer for about 20 minutes.
3. Drain the squash well and transfer into a bowl.
4. With a potato masher, mash the squash well.
5. Add flour, eggs, milk, cheese and 3 tbsp of butter and mix until well combined.
6. Transfer the mixture into the prepared casserole dish.
7. Cook in the oven for about 30 minutes.
8. Meanwhile, in a bowl, mix together the remaining butter and cracker crumbs.
9. Remove the casserole dish from oven and sprinkle with the cracker crumb evenly.
10. Cook in the oven for about 10 minutes more.

Citrus Pastry Soufflé

🥣 Prep Time: 15 mins
🕐 Total Time: 1 hr 10 mins

Servings per Recipe: 8
Calories   465.3
Fat   33.1g
Cholesterol   270.9mg
Sodium   385.4mg
Carbohydrates   27.0g
Protein   15.0g

Ingredients

Filling:
8 oz. cream cheese
15 oz. ricotta cheese
2 egg yolks
1 tbsp sugar
1 tsp vanilla
Pastry
1/2 C. butter, softened
1/3 C. sugar
6 eggs
1 C. all-purpose flour
2 tsp baking powder
1 1/2 C. Greek yogurt
1/2 C. orange juice
Garnish
fresh sweetened fruit (berries)

Directions

1. Set your oven to 350 degrees F before doing anything else and grease a 9x13x2-inch glass baking dish.
2. For the filling: in a small bowl, add the cream cheese and beat until smooth.
3. Add the egg yolks, ricotta cheese, sugar and vanilla extract and mix until well combined.
4. For blintz: in a large bowl, add the butter and sugar and beat until creamy.
5. Add eggs and beat until well combined. In a third bowl, mix together the flour and baking powder. In a fourth bowl, mix together the yogurt and orange juice.
6. Add alternately into the egg mixture and mix until well combined.
7. Place half of the mixture into the prepared baking dish and top with the filling mixture evenly. Place the remaining mixture over the filling evenly.
8. Cook in the oven for about 45-55 minutes.
9. Remove from the oven and keep onto a wire rack to cool for about 15 minutes before cutting.
10. Serve with fresh sweetened fruit.

TOMATO
& Chives Soufflé

Prep Time: 20 mins
Total Time: 32 mins

Servings per Recipe: 4
Calories 106.5
Fat 3.8g
Cholesterol 124.5mg
Sodium 93.9mg
Carbohydrates 12.7g
Protein 6.1g

Ingredients

4 large tomatoes, halved and seeded
3 egg yolks
2 tbsp breadcrumbs
1 tbsp chives
2 egg whites, beaten

Directions

1. Set your oven to 375 degrees F before doing anything else.
2. Carefully, scoop out the pulp from each tomato half and reserve the tomato half shells.
3. Then, chop the tomato pulp very finely.
4. In a large bowl, add the chopped tomatoes, breadcrumbs and egg yolks and mix well.
5. Gently, fold in beaten egg whites.
6. Carefully, spoon the tomato pulp mixture into each tomato shell evenly.
7. Arrange filled tomato shells in a flat, oven-proof baking dish.
8. Cook in the oven for about 12 minutes.
9. Remove from the oven and serve immediately with the sprinkling of chives.

Carolina Grits Soufflé

Prep Time: 30 mins
Total Time: 2 hrs

Servings per Recipe: 12
Calories 273.0
Fat 18.5g
Cholesterol 102.9mg
Sodium 251.7mg
Carbohydrates 16.0g
Protein 10.4g

Ingredients

1 1/2 C. regular grits, cooked
1 tsp onion salt
1 tsp garlic salt
3/4 tsp Worcestershire sauce
1/2 C. butter
3 eggs, slightly beaten
3/4 lb. cheddar cheese, shredded
paprika

Directions

1. In a large bowl, add the cooked grits, onion salt, garlic salt, Worcestershire sauce and butter and mix until well combined.
2. Add the beaten eggs and cheese and stir combine.
3. Transfer the mixture into a 2 1/2-quart baking dish and sprinkle with the paprika generously.
4. Refrigerate, covered overnight.
5. Set your oven to 350 degrees F.
6. Remove from the refrigerator and keep aside for at least 15 minutes before baking.
7. Cook in the oven for about 1 1/2 hours.

CRAB
& Egg Soufflé

Prep Time: 15 mins
Total Time: 1 hr

Servings per Recipe: 6
Calories   292.7
Fat   23.8g
Cholesterol   467.4mg
Sodium   649.6mg
Carbohydrates   2.9g
Protein   16.1g

Ingredients

12 eggs
1/2 C. milk
1 tsp salt
1/2 tsp white pepper
1/2 tsp dried dill
1 C. crab

8 oz. cream cheese, cubed
paprika
butter, melted for ramekins

Directions

1. Set your oven to 350 degrees F before doing anything else and grease 6 ramekins with the melted butter.
2. Ina bowl, add the milk, eggs, dill, salt and pepper and beat until well combined.
3. Add the crab and cheese and gently, stir to combine.
4. Place the mixture into the prepared ramekins evenly and sprinkle with the paprika.
5. Cook in the oven for about 40 - 45 minutes.

Minced Rice Soufflé

Prep Time: 20 mins
Total Time: 1 hr 5 mins

Servings per Recipe: 6
Calories   302.3
Fat   18.1g
Cholesterol   154.1mg
Sodium   472.9mg
Carbohydrates   20.4g
Protein   13.9g

Ingredients

- 2 tbsp butter
- 2 tbsp all-purpose flour
- 1 1/2 C. milk
- 2 C. cooked long-grain rice
- 1 1/2 C. shredded sharp cheddar cheese
- 1 tbsp minced green onion
- 1 tbsp minced fresh parsley
- 1/2 tsp salt
- 1 tsp Worcestershire sauce
- 1/4 tsp Tabasco sauce
- 3 eggs, separated

Directions

1. In a heavy pan, melt the butter over low heat and stir in the flour until smooth.
2. Cook for about 1 minute, stirring continuously.
3. Slowly, stir in the milk and cook until mixture becomes thick.
4. Add the remaining ingredients except the egg and stir to combine.
5. Remove from the heat and keep aside to cool completely.
6. In a bowl, add the egg yolks and with an electric mixer, beat on high speed until thick and lemon colored.
7. Add the egg yolks into the rice mixture and stir well.
8. In another bowl, add the egg whites and beat until stiff peaks form.
9. Fold 1/3 of the beaten egg whites into rice mixture.
10. Gently, fold in the remaining egg whites.
11. Place the rice mixture into an ungreased 1-1/2-quart casserole dish.
12. Cook in the oven for about 45-60 minutes.
13. Remove from the oven and serve immediately.

KETOGENIC
Soufflé

🍲 Prep Time: 10 mins
⏰ Total Time: 50 mins

Servings per Recipe: 6
Calories   477.1
Fat   42.8g
Cholesterol   282.8mg
Sodium   634.3mg
Carbohydrates   3.7g
Protein   19.7g

Ingredients

5 eggs
1/2 C. heavy cream
1/4 C. grated Parmesan cheese
1/2 tsp prepared mustard
1/4 tsp salt
1/4 tsp ground black pepper

1/2 lb. cheddar cheese, cut into about 1-inch pieces
11 oz. cream cheese, cut into about 1-inch pieces

Directions

1. Set your oven to 375 degrees F before doing anything else and grease a large soufflé dish.
2. In a blender, add the eggs, Parmesan, cream, mustard, salt and black pepper and pulse until smooth.
3. While the motor is running, slowly add the cheddar and pulse until well combined.
4. While the motor is running, slowly add the cream cheese and pulse until well combined.
5. Place the mixture into the prepared soufflé dish evenly.
6. Cook in the oven for about 40-50 minutes.

Soufflé Bites

Prep Time: 30 mins
Total Time: 1 hr 15 mins

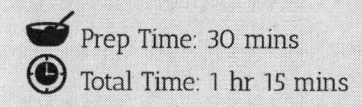

Servings per Recipe: 2
Calories 212.5
Fat 13.9g
Cholesterol 123.5mg
Sodium 96.5mg
Carbohydrates 15.2g
Protein 3.2g

Ingredients

- 2 tbsp unsalted butter, cut into pieces, more
- unsalted butter, for the ramekins
- granulated sugar, for dusting
- 1 tbsp water
- 1/2 tsp espresso powder
- 2 oz. bittersweet chocolate, finely chopped
- 1 pinch table salt
- 1 large egg, separated and at room temperature
- 1/4 C. confectioners' sugar

Directions

1. Set your oven to 400 degrees F before doing anything else. Lightly, grease 2 (6-oz.) ramekins with some butter and dust with granulated sugar, tapping out excess. Arrange the ramekins onto a small baking sheet.
2. In a small bowl, mix together the espresso powder and water. Keep aside until the coffee is dissolved, stirring occasionally.
3. In a microwave-safe bowl, add the chocolate and butter and microwave until melted completely. Remove from the microwave and beat the mixture until glossy and smooth.
4. Stir in the coffee mixture and salt. Add the egg yolks, one at a time, beating continuously until well combined. Add about 1/3 of the confectioners' sugar and beat until smooth.
5. In a medium bowl, add the egg whites and with an electric mixer, beat on medium-high speed until foamy and they're just beginning to hold soft peaks.
6. Increase the speed to high and slowly, add the remaining confectioners' sugar, beating continuously until firm peaks are formed. Place about 1/4 of the beaten whites into the chocolate mixture and beat until well combined. Gently fold in the remaining whites.
7. Transfer the mixture into the prepared ramekins evenly. Arrange the ramekins onto a baking sheet and cook in the oven for about 15 minute.
8. Remove from the oven and serve immediately.

SWISS CHOCOLATE
Soufflé

Prep Time: 1 hr
Total Time: 1 hr 30 mins

Servings per Recipe: 6
Calories 368.6
Fat 30.6g
Cholesterol 138.2mg
Sodium 172.9mg
Carbohydrates 27.5g
Protein 11.2g

Ingredients

2 tbsp unsalted butter
2 tbsp all-purpose flour
1 C. whole milk
8 oz. toblerone chocolate, dark chocolate
1 oz. unsweetened chocolate, chopped
3 tbsp honey
4 large eggs, separated
1/4 tsp salt
1 tbsp sugar
sliced almonds
powdered sugar

Directions

1. Grease 6 (1 1/4-C.) soufflé dishes and dust each with some sugar.
2. Arrange the soufflé dishes onto a large baking sheet.
3. In a heavy medium pan, melt the butter over medium heat.
4. stir in the flour and cook for about 2 minutes, beating continuously.
5. Increase the heat to medium-high.
6. Slowly, add the milk, beating continuously.
7. Cook for about 1 minute, beating continuously.
8. Remove from the heat and add honey, 6 oz. of the toblerone chocolate and unsweetened chocolate, beating continuously until melted and smooth.
9. Transfer the mixture into a large bowl and keep aside at room temperature to cool completely, stirring occasionally.
10. Set your oven to 450 degrees F.
11. Add the yolks into the chocolate mixture and beat until well combined.
12. In another bowl, add the egg whites and salt and beat until soft peaks form.
13. Add 1 tbsp of the sugar and beat until stiff and glossy.

14. Fold 1/4 of the whipped egg whites into chocolate mixture.
15. Gently fold in remaining egg whites.
16. Divide half of the mixture into the prepared soufflé dishes and top with 2 oz. of the chopped chocolate evenly.
17. Place the remaining mixture over chocolate in each dish and sprinkle with the almonds.
18. Cook in the oven for about 17 minutes.
19. Remove from the oven and serve immediately with a sifting of the powdered sugar.

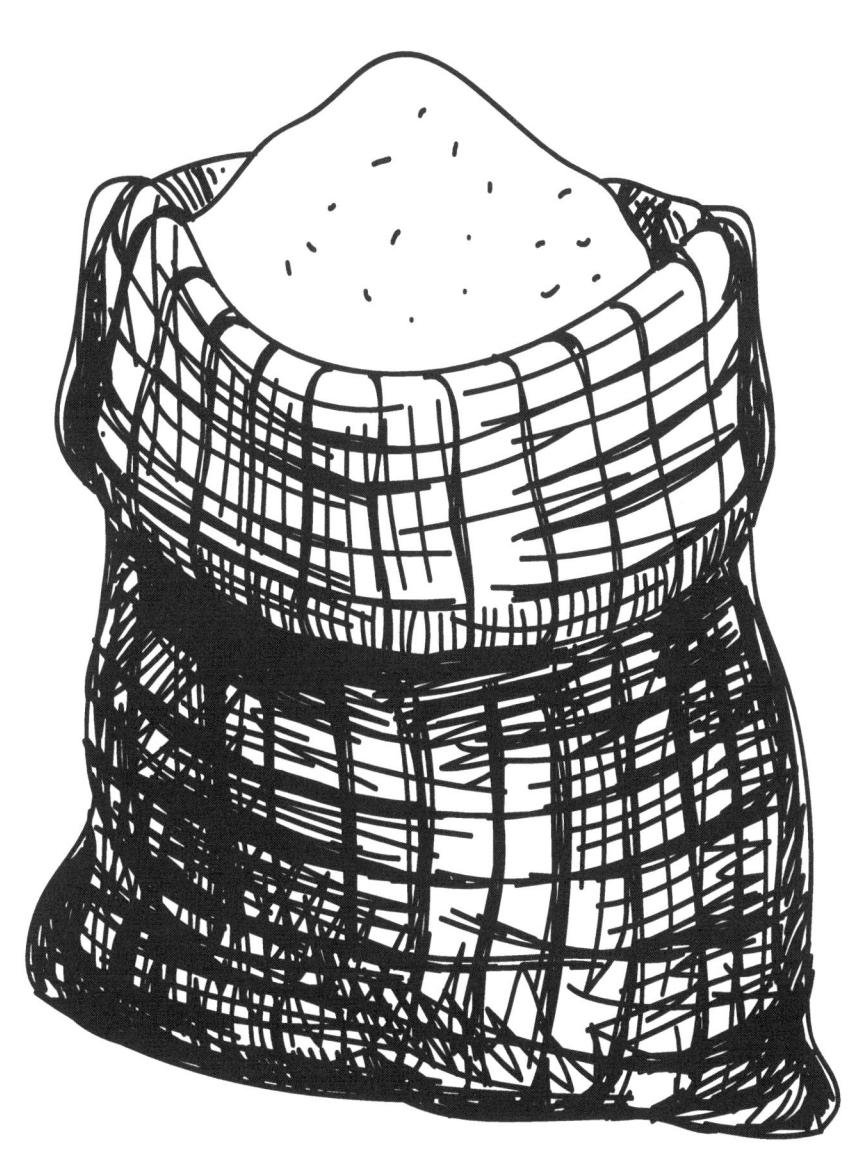

CHINESE
Soufflé

🥣 Prep Time: 15 mins
🕐 Total Time: 4 hrs 14 mins

Servings per Recipe: 6
Calories 324.8
Fat 16.3g
Cholesterol 115.8mg
Sodium 22.2mg
Carbohydrates 43.6g
Protein 3.1g

Ingredients

1 1/4 C. orange juice (preferably from concentrate, thawed and diluted)
1 (1 tbsp) envelope unflavored gelatin
1 C. sugar
2 large egg yolks

1 1/2 tbsp fresh lemon juice
1 C. heavy cream
1/2 C. canned mandarin orange section

Directions

1. For the custard: in a small bowl, dissolve the gelatin into orange juice and keep aside to let the gelatin soften.
2. In a small, heavy-bottomed pan, mix together the remaining orange juice, sugar and egg yolks over medium heat and cook until mixture becomes slightly thick, stirring continuously.
3. Add the softened gelatin mixture and lemon juice and stir to combine well.
4. Transfer the custard into a clean bowl and arrange in a large bowl of ice bath to cool, stirring occasionally.
5. In another bowl, add the heavy cream and with an electric whisk, beat until soft peaks form.
6. Gently, fold some whipped cream into the cooled custard.
7. Now, fold in remaining whipped cream into the cooled custard.
8. In the bottom of 6 (5-oz.) fluted plastic dessert molds, arrange 3-4 of the mandarin orange sections.
9. now, place the custard mixture over orange sections evenly.
10. Arrange the molds onto a baking sheet and with a plastic wrap, cover the molds.
11. Refrigerate to chill for at least 4 hours to overnight before serving.
12. Carefully unmold and serve.

Goat Cheese and Chives Soufflé

Prep Time: 10 mins
Total Time: 25 mins

Servings per Recipe: 4
Calories   240.1
Fat   18.8g
Cholesterol   347.2mg
Sodium   687.5mg
Carbohydrates   1.5g
Protein   15.7g

Ingredients

- 6 large eggs, separated
- 1/4 C. chopped fresh chives
- 1 tsp kosher salt
- 1/4 tsp black pepper
- 1 tbsp unsalted butter
- 4 oz. goat cheese

Directions

1. Set your oven to 400 degrees F before doing anything else.
2. In a large bowl, add the egg yolks, chives, salt, and pepper and beat until well combined.
3. In another bowl, add the egg whites and with an electric mixer, beat on medium-high speed until stiff peaks form.
4. Gently, fold the egg whites into the yolk mixture.
5. Meanwhile, in a large nonstick skillet, melt the butter over medium-low heat and tilt to coat the sides.
6. Place the soufflé mixture evenly and crumble the cheese on top.
7. transfer the skillet into the oven and cook for about 10 minutes.
8. Remove from the oven and cut into wedges before serving.

5-INGREDIENT Soufflé

Prep Time: 30 mins
Total Time: 1 hr 15 mins

Servings per Recipe: 8
Calories   197.1
Fat   7.9g
Cholesterol   171.7mg
Sodium   851.6mg
Carbohydrates   19.4g
Protein   11.5g

Ingredients

4 C. mashed potatoes, instant (prepared as pkg. directed)
6 eggs, separated
1 C. Parmesan cheese, shredded

1 tsp salt
1 tsp cream of tartar

Directions

1. Set your oven to 375 degrees F before doing anything else.
2. Prepare the instant mashed potatoes according to package's instructions.
3. Transfer the hot potatoes into a bowl.
4. Add the egg yolks, one at a time and mix until well combined.
5. Add the cheese and mix well.
6. Cover the bowl and keep aside at room temperature for a few hours.
7. In a bowl, add the egg whites and beat until foamy.
8. Add the cream of tartar and salt and beat until soft peaks form.
9. Gently, fold the whites into potato mixture.
10. Pace the mixture into a 4-quart soufflé dish evenly.
11. Cook in the oven for about 1 hour.

Southwest Soufflé

Prep Time: 15mins
Total Time: 55 mins

Servings per Recipe: 8
Calories	391.5
Fat	28.0g
Cholesterol	326.1mg
Sodium	1010.3mg
Carbohydrates	10.1g
Protein	24.1g

Ingredients

- 1/2 C. butter, melted
- 1/2 C. flour
- 1 tsp baking powder
- 1 tsp salt
- 10 large eggs
- 1 lb. low-fat small-curd cottage cheese
- 8 oz. canned diced green chiles
- 8 oz. Monterey Jack cheese, shredded

Directions

1. Set your oven to 350 degrees F before doing anything else and grease a 13x9-inch baking dish.
2. owl, mix together the flour, baking powder and salt.
3. Add the butter and mix until well combined.
4. In another bowl, add the eggs and beat well.
5. Add the remaining ingredients and mix well.
6. Add the egg mixture into the flour mixture and gently, stir to combine.
7. Place the mixture into the prepared baking dish.
8. Cook in the oven for about 40 minutes..

CAULIFLOWER
Soufflé

🥣 Prep Time: 40 mins
⏱ Total Time: 1 hr 10 mins

Servings per Recipe: 8
Calories 318.3
Fat 23.1g
Cholesterol 119.9mg
Sodium 740.4mg
Carbohydrates 11.3g
Protein 17.1g

Ingredients

1 head cauliflower
1/3 C. butter
1 1/3 C. milk
1/3 C. flour
1/3 C. whipping cream
2 eggs, separated

2 1/2 C. grated Parmesan cheese
1/2 tsp salt
1/4 tsp nutmeg

Directions

1. Set your oven to 325 degrees F before doing anything else and grease a 1-quart baking dish.
2. In the pan of the boiling salted water, add the cauliflower and cook, covered for about 4 minutes.
3. Drain the cauliflower and chop finely.
4. In a pan, melt the butter.
5. Add the flour and stir until smooth.
6. Reduce the heat to low and stir in the cream and milk.
7. Cook until mixture becomes slightly thick, stirring continuously.
8. Remove from the heat and stir in the nutmeg, salt and cheese, (reserving 2 tbsp).
9. Keep aside to cool. Meanwhile, in a bowl, add the egg whites and beat well.
10. Fold cauliflower into cream mixture. Add a little cream mixture and stir to combine.
11. Fold in beaten yolks. Then, fold in the egg whites.
12. Place the mixture into the prepared baking dish evenly and sprinkle with reserved cheese.
13. Cook in the oven for about 30 minutes.

Watercress Lemon Soufflé

Prep Time: 15 mins
Total Time: 50 mins

Servings per Recipe: 8
Calories	186.2
Fat	13.7g
Cholesterol	114.8mg
Sodium	175.9mg
Carbohydrates	6.5g
Protein	10.0g

Ingredients

- 12 oz. fresh spinach, washed and stems removed
- 1 bunch watercress, washed and stems removed
- 4 tbsp unsalted butter
- 3 tbsp all-purpose flour
- 1 1/4 C. milk
- 1/8 tsp ground nutmeg
- 4 oz. goat cheese (soft type)
- 4 egg yolks
- 1 tbsp fresh parsley, chopped
- 2 tsp fresh chives, chopped
- 6 egg whites
- 4 drops lemon juice
- salt and pepper, to taste

Directions

1. In a pan, add the spinach and watercress over medium heat and cook for about 3 minutes.
2. Drain the greens well and squeeze in a kitchen towel to release moisture.
3. Then, chop the greens roughly and keep aside.
4. Set your oven to 400 degrees F before doing anything else and grease a 2-quart round soufflé dish.
5. In a heavy pan, melt the butter over low heat.
6. Add the flour and beat until smooth.
7. Add the milk, nutmeg, salt and pepper and beat until well combined.
8. Increase the heat to medium and cook for about 2 minutes, stirring continuously.
9. Add the goat cheese and beat until smooth.
10. Remove from the heat and keep aside to cool slightly.
11. In a bowl, add the egg yolks and beat until lemon-colored.
12. Add 1/4 C. of the cooled sauce into egg yolks and beat until well combined.
13. Slowly, add the egg yolk mixture into the cool sauce and beat until well combined.

14. Stir in the spinach mixture, parsley and chives.
15. In a bowl, add the egg whites and lemon juice and with an electric mixer, beat the until frothy.
16. Then, beat continuously until stiff but not dry.
17. With a rubber spatula, gently fold 1/4 of the egg whites into the sauce.
18. Gently fold the remaining whites into the sauce until well combined.
19. Place the mixture into the prepared soufflé dish.
20. Cook in the oven for about 30 minutes.
21. Remove from the oven and serve immediately.

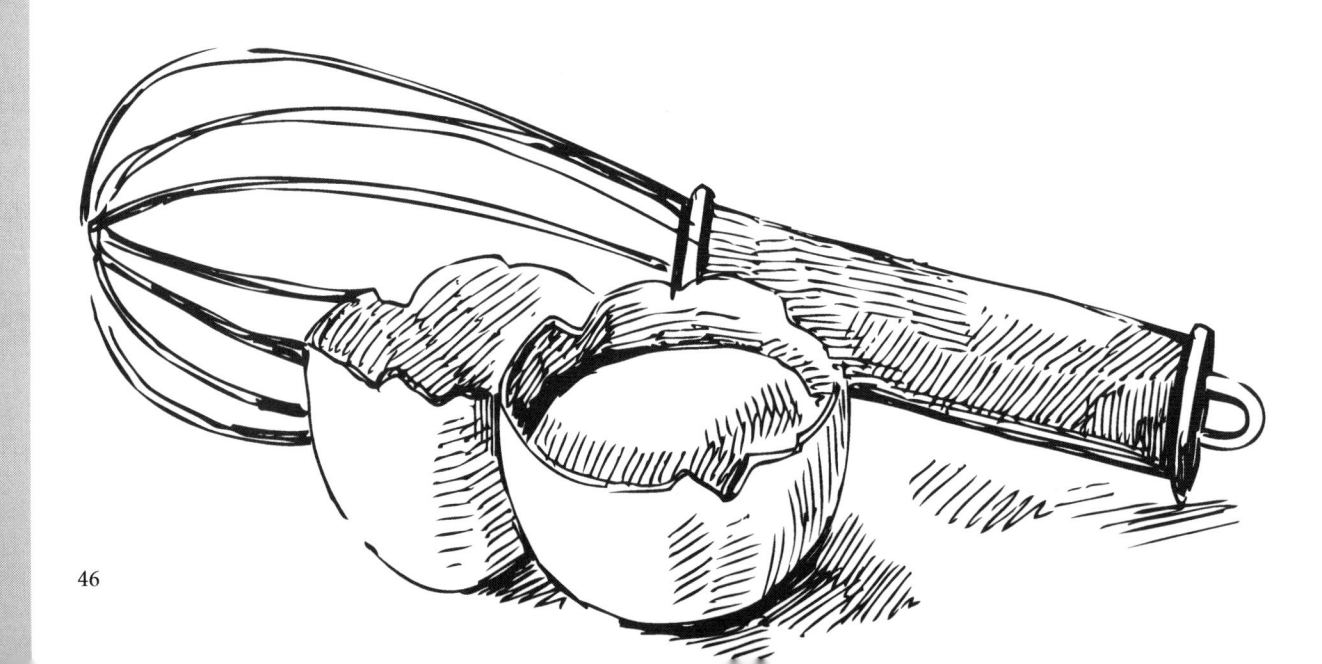

Hot Corn Soufflé

Prep Time: 5 mins
Total Time: 35 mins

Servings per Recipe: 8
Calories   516.9
Fat   37.7g
Cholesterol   353.6mg
Sodium   1004.5mg
Carbohydrates   14.4g
Protein   30.5g

Ingredients

- 1/2 C. flour
- 1 tsp baking powder
- 10 eggs, beaten lightly
- 1/2 C. butter, melted
- 4 C. grated Monterey Jack cheese
- 2 C. small curd cottage cheese
- 1 (4 oz.) cans diced green chilies
- 1 (8 oz.) cans canned corn, drained
- 1 dash salt & pepper

Directions

1. Set your oven to 400 degrees F before doing anything else and grease a 9x14-inch glass baking dish.
2. In a bowl, mix together the flour and baking powder.
3. Add the eggs and butter and mix until well combined.
4. Place the mixture into the prepared baking dish evenly.
5. Cook in the oven for about 30 minutes.

SPICER SPINACH
Soufflé

Prep Time: 20 mins
Total Time: 50 mins

Servings per Recipe: 4
Calories   268.2
Fat   20.0g
Cholesterol   303.4mg
Sodium   494.4mg
Carbohydrates   10.8g
Protein   11.0g

Ingredients

4 tbsp butter
1/4 C. flour
5 eggs, separated
1/3 C. grated onion
2/3 C. cooked spinach
1 C. milk

1/2 tsp Celtic sea salt
1/4 tsp cayenne pepper
1/2 seasoning salt

Directions

1. Set your oven to 350 degrees F before doing anything else and grease a 8x8-inch glass baking dish.
2. In a microwave-safe bowl, add the milk and microwave for about 2 minutes.
3. In a 10-inch non-stick skillet, melt the butter over medium-low heat.
4. Slowly, add the flour, stirring continuously until thick and smooth.
5. Add the milk and seasonings, stirring continuously until thick and smooth.
6. Add the spinach and onion and stir to combine.
7. Remove from the heat and immediately, stir in the yolks.
8. Transfer the mixture into a large glass bowl and keep aside.
9. In a bowl, add the egg whites and beat until stiff peaks form.
10. Add 1/3 of egg whites mixture into the spinach mixture and gently, stir to combine.
11. Fold in the remaining egg whites.
12. Place the mixture into prepared baking dish evenly.
13. Cook in the oven for about 30 minutes.
14. Remove from the oven and serve immediately.

Leftover Soufflé

Prep Time: 5 mins
Total Time: 35 mins

Servings per Recipe: 6
Calories   434.1
Fat   16.6g
Cholesterol   116.7mg
Sodium   337.8mg
Carbohydrates   54.6g
Protein   14.9g

Ingredients

- 2 tbsp butter
- 1 1/4 C. cheddar cheese, shredded
- 2 C. milk, hot
- 2 C. white rice, cooked
- 1/4 tsp salt
- 1/4 tsp dry mustard
- 2 eggs, slightly beaten
- paprika (optional)

Directions

1. Set your oven to 350 degrees F before doing anything else and grease a 9x9-inch shallow casserole dish.
2. In a bowl, add the cheese, butter and milk and beat until well combined.
3. Add the cooked rice, mustard and salt and mix well.
4. Add the beaten eggs and gently, stir to combine.
5. Place the mixture into the prepared casserole dish evenly and sprinkle with the paprika.
6. Cook in the oven for about 30 minutes.

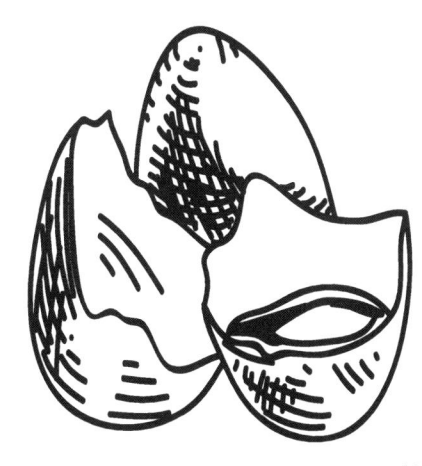

SUN-DRIED Tomato Soufflé

Prep Time: 25 mins
Total Time: 1 hr

Servings per Recipe: 8
Calories   234.6
Fat   14.0g
Cholesterol   110.6mg
Sodium   561.1mg
Carbohydrates   15.3g
Protein   11.5g

Ingredients

1 C. fine fresh breadcrumb
3 tbsp butter
3 tbsp all-purpose flour
3/4 C. milk
8 oz. feta cheese, crumbled
3 large egg yolks
3 tbsp minced sun-dried tomatoes (packed in oil and drained)
1 tbsp minced fresh dill
7 large egg whites
salad greens
vinaigrette

Directions

1. Set your oven to 375 degrees F before doing anything else and arrange a rack in the middle of the oven.
2. Grease 8 (1/2 C.) ramekins with some butter and coat with the breadcrumbs evenly, shaking off the excess and reserving them.
3. For the roux: in a medium pan, melt the butter over medium-low heat.
4. Add the flour, beating continuously.
5. Cook for about 3 minutes, beating continuously.
6. Slowly, add the milk in a stream, beating continuously and then, bring to a boil.
7. Immediately, remove from the heat.
8. In a large bowl, add the roux mixture, 3/4 C. of the cheese, egg yolks, sun-dried tomatoes, dill, and salt and beat until well combined.
9. In another bowl, add the egg whites and beat until stiff peaks form.
10. Gently, fold the whipped whites into cheese mixture in 2 portions.
11. Place the mixture in each ramekin about halfway through and top with the remaining cheese, followed by the remaining soufflé mixture and top with reserved crumbs.
12. Arrange the ramekins into a large roasting pan.

13. In the roasting pan, add enough hot water to reach halfway up sides of ramekins.
14. Cook in the oven for about 25 minutes.
15. Remove from the oven and keep aside onto a wire rack for about 15 minutes.
16. Carefully, cut around around the edge of the soufflés and invert them.
17. With a plastic wrap, cover the soufflés and refrigerate up to 6 hours.
18. Remove from the refrigerator and bring to room temperature before further baking.
19. Set you oven to 425 degrees F and arrange a rack in the middle of the oven.
20. Cook in the oven for about 5-7 minutes.
21. Divide salad into 8 serving plates and top each serving with one soufflé.
22. Serve immediately.

MILKY WHITE
Soufflé

Prep Time: 30 mins
Total Time: 50 mins

Servings per Recipe: 8
Calories   208.5
Fat   7.4g
Cholesterol   119.4mg
Sodium   139.6mg
Carbohydrates   28.0g
Protein   6.9g

Ingredients

2 tbsp unsalted butter
1/3 C. granulated sugar, plus more for dishes
2 C. whole milk
1/2 vanilla bean, split lengthwise and scraped
3/4 C. flour, plus
2 tbsp all-purpose flour
1/4 tsp salt
4 large eggs, separated
1 tsp pure vanilla extract
1 large egg white
1/4 C. sugar
1/4 tsp cream of tartar
confectioners' sugar, for dusting
vanilla ice cream

Directions

1. For the soufflé base: in a medium pan, add the milk and vanilla bean with scrapings over high heat and bring to a boil.
2. Remove from the heat and keep aside, covered for 1 hour.
3. Remove the bean from milk.
4. In a medium bowl, mix together the flour, 1/3 C. of the granulated sugar and salt.
5. Add 1/2 C. of the steeped milk and beat until a sooth paste is formed.
6. Transfer the paste into the pan with the remaining milk over medium heat and cook for about 5-8 minutes, beating continuously.
7. Remove from the heat and beat until smooth.
8. Add the egg yolks and vanilla extract and beat until well combined.
9. Transfer the mixture into a 1-quart shallow container.
10. With a plastic wrap, cover the surface directly.
11. Arrange the pan in the ice-water bath to cool completely.

12. Refrigerate until using.
13. Remove the soufflé base from refrigerator and keep side at room temperature for about 1 hour before using.
14. Set your oven to 375 degrees F and arrange a rack in the center of oven.
15. Grease 8 (6-oz.) soufflé dishes with the butter and then, dust inside and rims of of each dish with the sugar.
16. In the bowl of an electric mixer, fitted with the whisk attachment, add 5 egg whites and cream of tartar and beat on low speed until foamy.
17. Slowly, add remaining 1/4 C. of the sugar, while slowly increasing the speed of the mixer until it is on high and beat until egg whites are stiff and shiny.
18. In three portions, gently fold egg whites into the soufflé base.
19. Divide the mixture into the prepared soufflé dishes evenly and gently, tap dish on to a counter top.
20. Arrange the soufflé dishes onto a baking sheet.
21. Cook in the oven for about 16-20 minutes.
22. Remove from the oven and dust with the confectioners' sugar.
23. Serve immediately alongside the vanilla bean ice cream.

SOUFFLÉ
in its Simplest

Prep Time: 1 hr
Total Time: 1 hr 30 mins

Servings per Recipe: 3
Calories	330.6
Fat	21.2g
Cholesterol	175.3mg
Sodium	1365.2mg
Carbohydrates	17.9g
Protein	16.9g

Ingredients

- 2 slices bread, trimmed
- 1 tbsp butter
- 1 C. cheese, grated
- 2 eggs, beaten
- 1 1/2 C. milk
- 1 tsp salt
- 1 tsp pepper

Directions

1. Grease a deep baking dish with some melted butter.
2. Spread the butter onto both sides of the bread slices.
3. In a bowl, add the milk and eggs and beat until well combined.
4. Arrange the buttered bread slices in the bottom of the prepared baking dish and sprinkle with the cheese.
5. Place the egg mixture over the cheese and sprinkle with the salt and pepper.
6. Keep aside for about 1 hour.
7. Set your oven to 350 degrees F.
8. arrange the baking dish in a large roasting pan.
9. In the roasting pan, add enough water to come half way through of the baking dish.
10. Cook in the oven for about 30 minutes.

Maple Soufflé

🥣 Prep Time: 24 hrs
🕐 Total Time: 24 hrs 50 mins

Servings per Recipe: 8
Calories   752.2
Fat   55.1g
Cholesterol   377.3mg
Sodium   524.3mg
Carbohydrates   51.8g
Protein   14.8g

Ingredients

4 -5 medium croissants (baked)
8 oz. cream cheese, softened
4 oz. butter, softened
3/4 C. maple syrup, divided
10 eggs
3 C. half-and-half milk
1 tsp ground cinnamon
powdered sugar
chopped pecans
Topping:
4 oz. butter
1/2 C. maple syrup

Directions

1. Chop the croissants roughly.
2. Divide the chopped croissants into a greased 13X9-inch casserole dish.
3. In a bowl, add the butter, cream cheese and 1/3 C. of the maple syrup ad mix until well combined.
4. In another large bowl, add the eggs, 1/2 C. of the maple syrup and half-and-half and beat until well combined.
5. Place the butter mixture over the chopped croissants evenly and top with the egg mixture. Sprinkle with the cinnamon and refrigerate, covered overnight.
6. Set your oven to 350 degrees F.
7. Uncover the casserole dish and cook in the oven for about 45-50 minutes.
8. Remove from the oven and keep onto a ire rack for about 5-10 minutes.
9. Meanwhile, for the sauce: in small pan, add 1/2 C. of the butter and 1/2 C. of the maple syrup and cook until heated through.
10. Remove from the heat and pour over the sauce over the warm soufflé evenly.
11. Serve with a topping of the powdered sugar and pecans.

CHIPOTLE
Soufflé

🥣 Prep Time: 5 mins
🕐 Total Time: 25 mins

Servings per Recipe: 4
Calories   136.7
Fat   4.7g
Cholesterol   186.0mg
Sodium   72.0mg
Carbohydrates   17.9g
Protein   6.3g

Ingredients

4 eggs
10 oz. Simply Potatoes Diced Potatoes with Onion
8 oz. cheddar cheese, shredded
1/4 C. honey
2 chipotle peppers, pulverized

Directions

1. In a small microwave-safe container, add the honey and pulverized chipotle peppers and microwave until honey is melted.
2. Keep aside for a few hours.
3. Through a trainer, strain the larger pieces of chipotle pepper.
4. Set your oven to 350 degrees F and grease 4 ramekins.
5. In a bowl, add the potatoes and eggs and with an immersion blender, blend until well combined.
6. Add the cheddar and stir to combine.
7. Divide the mixture into the prepared ramekins evenly.
8. Cook in the oven for about 20 minutes.

Big Apple Soufflé

Prep Time: 15 mins
Total Time: 55 mins

Servings per Recipe: 8
Calories   254.0
Fat   3.4g
Cholesterol   1.2mg
Sodium   304.3mg
Carbohydrates   46.8g
Protein   10.6g

Ingredients

- 1 C. all-purpose flour
- 2 tbsp all-purpose flour
- 3 tbsp sugar
- 1/2 tsp salt
- 1/2 tsp cinnamon
- 2 C. fat free egg substitute
- 2 C. skim milk
- 1 tsp vanilla extract
- 2 tbsp unsalted margarine
- 6 apples, peeled and sliced thin
- 3 tbsp light brown sugar, firmly packed

Directions

1. Set your oven to 425 degrees F before doing anything else.
2. In a large bowl, mix together the flour, sugar, cinnamon and salt.
3. Make a well in the center of flour mixture.
4. Add the milk, egg substitute and vanilla in the well and beat until well combined.
5. In a 13x9-inch baking dish, add the margarine.
6. Place the baking dish in the oven for about 3 minutes.
7. Add the apples and gently, stir to coat.
8. Cook in the oven for about 5 minutes.
9. Place the egg mixture over the apples evenly and sprinkle with the brown sugar.
10. Cook in the oven for about 5 minutes.
11. Remove from the oven and serve immediately.

WESTERN EUROPEAN
Soufflé

Prep Time: 20 mins
Total Time: 40 mins

Servings per Recipe: 4
Calories	361.3
Fat	19.4g
Cholesterol	83.1mg
Sodium	382.0mg
Carbohydrates	19.8g
Protein	26.3g

Ingredients

20 g butter
1 leek, sliced
20 g butter, extra
1/4 C. flour
1/3 C. water
375 ml carnation light & creamy evaporated milk
2 tbsp chopped parsley
210 g salmon, drained and flaked
salt & pepper
1/4 C. grated Parmesan cheese
6 egg whites

Directions

1. Set your oven to 390 degrees F before doing anything else and grease a 4 (1-C.) soufflé dishes.
2. In a pan, melt the butter and cook the leek for about 5 minutes.
3. Transfer the leek into a bowl and keep aside.
4. In the same pan, melt the extra butter.
5. Stir in the flour and water until smooth paste is formed.
6. Stir in the evaporated milk and bring to boil stirring continuously.
7. Remove from the heat and stir in the salmon, Parmesan, leek, parsley, salt and pepper.
8. Ina small bowl, add the egg whites and beat until stiff peaks form.
9. Fold the whipped egg whites into the soufflé mixture.
10. Divide the mixture into the prepared soufflé dishes evenly.
11. Cook in the oven for about 20 minutes.

How to Make a Soufflé

🥣 Prep Time: 10 mins
🕐 Total Time: 35 mins

Servings per Recipe: 6
Calories   272.1
Fat   14.5g
Cholesterol   109.0mg
Sodium   692.8mg
Carbohydrates   21.6g
Protein   13.8g

Ingredients

2 tbsp butter
3 medium sweet onions, chopped
5 slices fresh bread, cut into cubes
10 oz. evaporated milk
2 eggs, lightly beaten

1 C. shredded Parmesan cheese
1/2 tsp salt

Directions

1. Set your oven to 350 degrees F before doing anything else and lightly, grease a 1 1/2-quart soufflé dish.
2. In a large skillet, melt the butter over medium heat and sauté the onions for about 10-15 minutes.
3. Remove from the heat and transfer the onions into a large bowl.
4. Add the bread cubes, eggs, milk, 3/4 C. of the cheese and salt and stir to combine.
5. place the mixture into prepared soufflé dish and top with the remaining 1/4 C. of the cheese.
6. Cook in the oven for about 25 minutes.

BRAZILIAN
Fruit Soufflé

Prep Time: 15 mins
Total Time: 30 mins

Servings per Recipe: 4
Calories   140.9
Fat   1.3g
Cholesterol   52.4mg
Sodium   82.5mg
Carbohydrates   29.8g
Protein   4.0g

Ingredients

butter-flavored cooking spray
5 tbsp sugar
2 bananas
1 tbsp fresh lime juice
1 large egg yolk
3 large egg whites
1 pinch salt

Directions

1. Set your oven to 400 degrees F before doing anything else and arrange a rack in the center of the oven.
2. Lightly, grease a 4 (1-C.) ramekins with cooking spray.
3. Dust each raekin with 1/2 tablespoon of sugar
4. Shake and roll each ramekin to coat the bottom and sides evenly.
5. In a food processor, add the bananas, egg yolk, lime juice and 2 tbsp of the sugar and pulse until smooth.
6. Transfer the pureed mixture into a large bowl.
7. In a glass bowl, add the egg whites with a pinch of salt and beat until soft peaks form.
8. Add remaining 1 tbsp of the sugar and beat until glossy and firm.
9. With a rubber spatula, fold 1/4 the whipped whites into the banana mixture.
10. Now, gently fold in the remaining whites.
11. Divide the mixture into the prepared ramekins evenly and tap them lightly on a counter top to remove the air bubble.
12. Arrange ramekins onto a baking sheet and cook in the oven for about 15 minutes.
13. Remove from the oven and serve immediately.

Mint Cocoa Soufflé

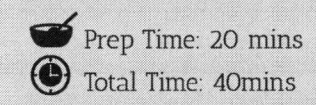

🥣 Prep Time: 20 mins
🕐 Total Time: 40mins

Servings per Recipe: 2
Calories   161.9
Fat   8.6g
Cholesterol   186.8mg
Sodium   168.1mg
Carbohydrates   15.5g
Protein   9.1g

Ingredients

2 eggs, separated, room temperature
1 tsp sugar (plus 4 tbsp, divided)
2 tbsp baking cocoa
1 tsp cornstarch
1 dash salt

1/3 C. nonfat milk
2 tbsp semi-sweet chocolate chips
1/8 tsp mint extract
confectioners' sugar

Directions

1. Set your oven to 375 degrees F before doing anything else and grease 2 (10-oz.) ramekins. Then, sprinkle the ramekins with 1 tsp of the sugar.
2. Arrange the ramekins onto a baking sheet and keep aside.
3. In a small pan, mix together 2 tbsp of the sugar, cocoa, cornstarch and salt over medium heat. Slowly, stir in milk and bring to a boil, stirring continuously.
4. Cook for about 1-2 minutes, stirring continuously.
5. Remove from the heat and stir in chocolate chips and mint extract until chips are melted completely. Transfer the chocolate mixture into a small bowl.
6. In a large bowl, place the egg yolks. Add small amount of hot chocolate mixture into egg yolks and stir to combine well. Slowly, add the remaining chocolate mixture into the bowl, stirring continuously. Keep aside to cool slightly.
7. In another bowl, add the egg whites and with n electric mixer, beat on medium speed until soft peaks form.
8. Slowly, add the remaining sugar, 1 tbsp at a time and beat on high speed until stiff peaks form.Gently, fold 1/4 of the whipped egg whites into chocolate mixture.
9. Gently, fold in the remaining egg whites. Place the mixture into the prepared ramekins.
10. Cook in the oven for about 18-22 minutes.
11. Remove from the oven and serve immediately with the sprinkling of confectioners' sugar.

SWEET Ricotta Soufflé

Prep Time: 15 mins
Total Time: 30 mins

Servings per Recipe: 4
Calories   123.8
Fat   7.2g
Cholesterol   112.0mg
Sodium   112.5mg
Carbohydrates   3.5g
Protein   10.1g

Ingredients

1 C. part-skim ricotta cheese
2 large eggs, separated
3 tbsp Splenda granular
2 tsp grated lemon zest
1/2 tsp lemon extract
1/2 tsp vanilla extract

Directions

1. Set your oven to 375 degrees F before doing anything else and grease 4 (4-oz.) ramekins.
2. In a large bowl, add the egg yolks, ricotta, 1 tbsp of the Splenda, lemon zest and both extracts and beat until well combined.
3. In another small bowl, add the egg whites and with an electric mixer, beat on high speed until soft peaks form.
4. Slowly, add remaining 2 tbsp of the Splenda and beat until stiff peaks form.
5. Gently, fold egg whites into the ricotta mixture.
6. Place the ricotta mixture into the prepared ramekins evenly.
7. Cook in the oven for about 15 minutes.
8. Remove from the oven and serve immediately.

Dry Mustard Soufflé

Prep Time: 1 hr 10 mins
Total Time: 2 hrs 10mins

Servings per Recipe: 4
Calories 594.6
Fat 38.8g
Cholesterol 292.5mg
Sodium 1111.6mg
Carbohydrates 27.4g
Protein 34.6g

Ingredients

5 slices bread, buttered and cubed
3/4 lb. sharp cheddar cheese, grated
4 eggs
2 C. milk
1/2 tsp salt
1/2 tsp dry mustard
1/2 tsp pepper

Directions

1. Grease a soufflé dish with some butter.
2. In a bowl, add the eggs, milk, mustard, salt and pepper and beat until well combined.
3. In the bottom of prepared soufflé dish, arrange bread slices and top with cheese slices.
4. Place the egg mixture on top evenly.
5. Keep aside at room temperature for about one hour.
6. Set your oven to 350 degrees F.
7. Cook in the oven for about one hour.

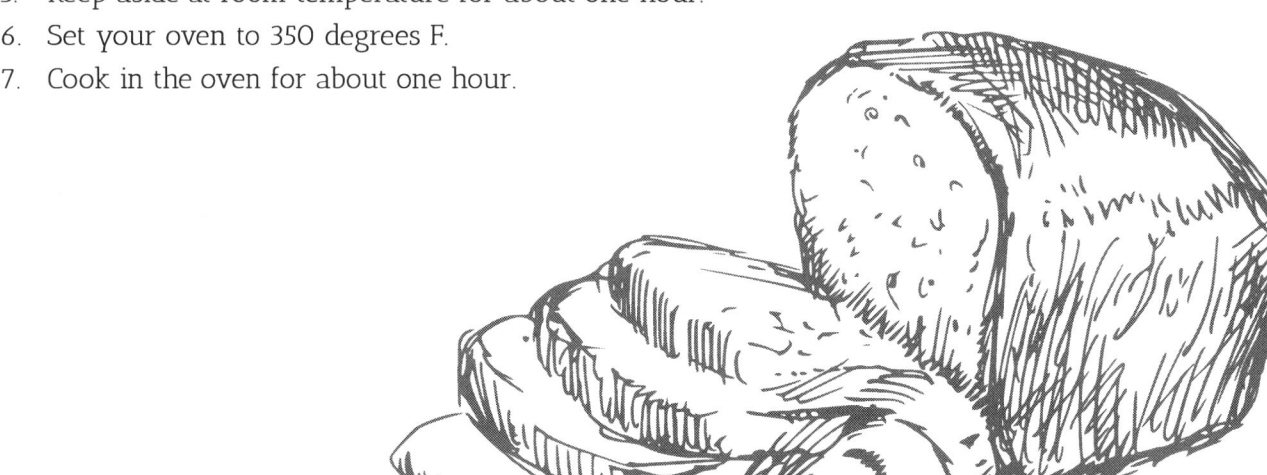

SPICY BELL
Mushroom Soufflé

Prep Time: 10 mins
Total Time: 20 mins

Servings per Recipe: 6
Calories   327.7
Fat   25.4g
Cholesterol   160.1mg
Sodium   565.0mg
Carbohydrates   8.1g
Protein   16.9g

Ingredients

1/4 C. butter
1/4 C. flour
1/2 tsp salt
1/4 tsp cayenne pepper
1 C. milk
8 oz. grated sharp cheddar cheese
3 egg yolks
6 -8 sliced mushrooms
2 tbsp diced red bell peppers
1/2 C. diced broccoli
2 tsp olive oil
6 egg whites
confectioners' sugar

Directions

1. Set your oven to 450 degrees F before doing anything else. For the roux: in a pan, melt the butter over medium heat.
2. Add the flour, salt and cayenne pepper and beat until well combined. Stir in the milk and cook until the mixture becomes thick.
3. Remove from the heat and stir in the cheese until melted. In another bowl, add the egg yolks and beat until thick and lemon colored. Slowly, add the whipped egg yolks into the cheese mixture, stirring continuously. Keep aside, covered to keep warm.
4. In a skillet, heat the oil and sauté the mushrooms, broccoli and red peppers until tender.
5. In a small bowl, add the egg whites and beat until stiff peaks form.
6. In another large bowl, add 2 C. of the roux and cooked vegetables and stir to combine.
7. Gently, fold in the whipped egg whites. Place the mixture into an ungreased soufflé dish.
8. Arrange the soufflé dish in a roasting pan. In the roasting pan, add enough hot water to come half way through soufflé dish. Cook in the oven for about 15-20 minutes.
9. Serve immediately with a sprinkling of the confectioners' sugar.

Buttery Challah Soufflé

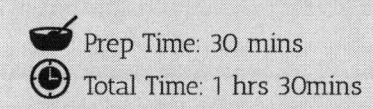

Prep Time: 30 mins
Total Time: 1 hrs 30mins

Servings per Recipe: 12
Calories   269.5
Fat   13.4g
Cholesterol   93.4mg
Sodium   452.3mg
Carbohydrates   27.4g
Protein   10.4g

Ingredients

1 lb mushroom, sliced
7-9 tbsp light butter
14 slices challah (egg bread)
1/2 C. celery, chopped
1/2 C. onion, chopped
1/2 C. green pepper, chopped
1/2 C. light mayonnaise
salt and pepper

3 eggs
1 1/2 C. skim milk
1 (10 3/4 oz.) cans low-fat cream of mushroom soup
1/2 C. Parmesan cheese, grated

Directions

1. In a skillet, melt 1-2 tbsp of the butter and sauté the mushrooms slightly.
2. Transfer the mushrooms into a bowl and keep aside.
3. In the same skillet, melt 1-2 tbsp of the butter and sauté the onion, celery and green pepper lightly.
4. Spread about 3 tbsp of the butter over 6 bread slices evenly and cut each into 1-inch cubes. Cut 4 remaining unbuttered bread slices into cubes.
5. In a bowl, mix together the sautéed vegetables, mushrooms, mayonnaise, salt and pepper.
6. In another bowl, add the milk and eggs and beat well.
7. In the bottom of a 9x13-inch baking dish, arrange the bread slices and top with the mushroom mixture evenly.
8. Top with the bread cubes evenly, followed by the egg mixture. Refrigerate, covered overnight. Set your oven to 325 degrees F.
9. Spread the bitter over remaining 4 bread slices and then cut into cubes.
10. Place the mushroom soup over the chilled mixture and top with the cheese.
11. Cook in the oven for about 1 hour.

AUGUST
Berry Soufflé

Prep Time: 20 mins
Total Time: 35 mins

Servings per Recipe: 6
Calories   133.1
Fat   0.1g
Cholesterol   0.0mg
Sodium   46.5mg
Carbohydrates   30.5g
Protein   3.3g

Ingredients

5 egg whites
butter
sugar
2 C. sliced fresh strawberries
1/4-1/3 C. sugar

4 tsp cornstarch
1/2 C. sugar
strawberry syrup

Directions

1. In a bowl, add the egg whites and keep aside at room temperature for about 30 minutes before using.
2. Grease 6 (1-C.) soufflé dishes with the butter and sprinkle with sugar, shaking out any excess.
3. Arrange the soufflé dishes onto a shallow baking sheet.
4. Meanwhile, in a bowl, mix together the strawberries and 1/4 to 1/3 C. of the sugar.
5. Keep aside for about 15 minutes.
6. In a food processor, add the strawberry mixture and cornstarch and pulse until smooth.
7. Set your oven to 350 degrees F.
8. In a large bowl, add the egg whites and beat until soft peaks form.
9. Slowly, add 1/2 C. of the sugar, beating continuously until stiff glossy peaks form.
10. With a rubber spatula, push the whipped egg whites to the side of the bowl.
11. Place the strawberry mixture into bottom of the bowl.
12. Carefully, stir a little of the beaten egg whites into the strawberry mixture.
13. Then, fold the both mixtures together.
14. Place the mixture into the prepared soufflé dishes evenly.
15. Cook in the oven for about 15-18 minutes.
16. Remove from the oven and serve immediately with a topping of the strawberry syrup.

Green Onion Swiss Shrimp Soufflé

Prep Time: 1 hr
Total Time: 1 hrs 30mins

Servings per Recipe: 4
Calories	782.1
Fat	38.3g
Cholesterol	626.7mg
Sodium	845.8mg
Carbohydrates	32.9g
Protein	68.6g

Ingredients

1/2 C. flour
2 C. milk
4 egg yolks
salt and pepper
2 dashes nutmeg
6 egg whites
1/2 C. Swiss cheese, grated
Filling:
1 C. green onion, chopped
4 tbsp butter
1/2 C. white wine
2 lb. shrimp, cleaned
1/2 C. mushroom, sliced
salt and pepper
Sauce For Filling (Use 1 C.)
2 tbsp butter
2 tbsp flour
2 C. milk
1 dash white pepper
1/4 tsp salt
1 dash nutmeg

Directions

1. Set your oven to 375 degrees F before doing anything else and line a jelly roll pan with a greased waxed paper and then, flour it.
2. For the bechamel sauce: in a heavy pan, melt the butter.
3. Add the flour and with a whisk, blend well.
4. Slowly, add the milk, beating continuously and cook until sauce becomes thick.
5. Stir in the nutmeg, salt and black pepper and remove from the heat.
6. For the soufflé: in a pan, add the milk and flour and cook until thick, stirring continuously.
7. Remove from the heat and add the egg yolks, one at a time, beating continuously until well combined.
8. Add the nutmeg, salt and black pepper and stir to combine.
9. In a large bowl, add the egg whites and beat well.

10. Fold the flour mixture into the whipped whites.
11. Add the cheese and stir to combine.
12. Place the mixture into the prepared jelly roll pan.
13. Cook in the oven for about 18-20 minutes.
14. For the shrimp filling: in a skillet, melt the butter and sauté the green onions until just tender.
15. Add the shrimp and wine and cook for about 5 minutes.
16. Add the mushrooms, salt and pepper and simmer for about 5 minutes.
17. remove from the heat and stir in 1 C. of the bechamel sauce.
18. Remove the pan from the oven and invert the soufflé onto a dampened kitchen towel.
19. Carefully, remove the waxed paper.
20. Place the shrimp filling over the soufflé and roll up like a jelly roll.
21. Serve alongside the remaining bechamel sauce.

Idaho Potato Soufflé

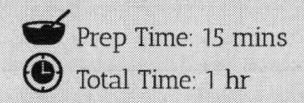

Prep Time: 15 mins
Total Time: 1 hr

Servings per Recipe: 4
Calories   140.3
Fat   2.7g
Cholesterol   8.4mg
Sodium   263.1mg
Carbohydrates   22.0g
Protein   7.0g

Ingredients

- 1 lb. potato, peeled and cut into large chunks
- 1 tbsp light margarine, softened
- 1/3 C. fat-free half-and-half, warmed
- 1/4 tsp sea salt
- 1/2 tsp fresh coarse ground black pepper
- 6 tbsp egg whites
- 1/4 C. sharp cheddar cheese, finely grated
- 1 tsp flaked sea salt

Directions

1. In a large pan of the water, add the potatoes and bring to a boil.
2. Cook for about 10-15 minutes or until tender.
3. Drain the potatoes well and return to pot over low heat.
4. Cook, covered for about 3 minutes, shaking the pan occasionally.
5. With an electric hand mixer, mash the potatoes on low speed.
6. Add the milk, butter, salt and black pepper and gently, stir to combine.
7. Keep aside to cool. Set your oven to 400 degrees F and grease an 8x8-inch baking dish.
8. In a small bowl, add 3 tbsp of the egg whites and beat well.
9. Add the beaten egg whites into the potatoes and stir to combine.
10. Add the cheese and stir to combine.
11. In another small bowl, add remaining 3 tbsp of the egg whites and with an electric hand mixer, beat until stiff peaks form.
12. Gently, fold the whipped egg whites into the potatoes.
13. Transfer the potato mixture into the prepared baking dish.
14. Cook in the oven for about 30 minutes.
15. Serve with a sprinkling of the flaked salt.

THAI
Curry Soufflé

🍲 Prep Time: 10 mins
🕒 Total Time: 40 mins

Servings per Recipe: 4
Calories   250.9
Fat   20.2g
Cholesterol   0.0mg
Sodium   22.2mg
Carbohydrates   10.9g
Protein   10.6g

Ingredients

1/2 red bell pepper, julienned
1 green onion, chopped
10 Thai basil leaves, julienned
1 (16 oz.) packages firm tofu
1 C. coconut milk
6 tbsp panang curry paste

2 tbsp sugar
1 tbsp vegetable oil
salt
pepper

Directions

1. Set your oven to 350 degrees F before doing anything else.
2. In a frying pan, heat the oil and sauté the onion and bell pepper for about 5 minutes.
3. In a food processor, add the tofu, sugar, coconut milk, curry paste, salt and pepper and pulse until smooth.
4. Transfer the pureed mixture into a soufflé dish.
5. Add the sautéed onion mixture and basil and stir to combine.
6. Arrange the soufflé dish in a roasting pan that is filled half way with water.
7. Cook in the oven for about 30 - 45 minutes.

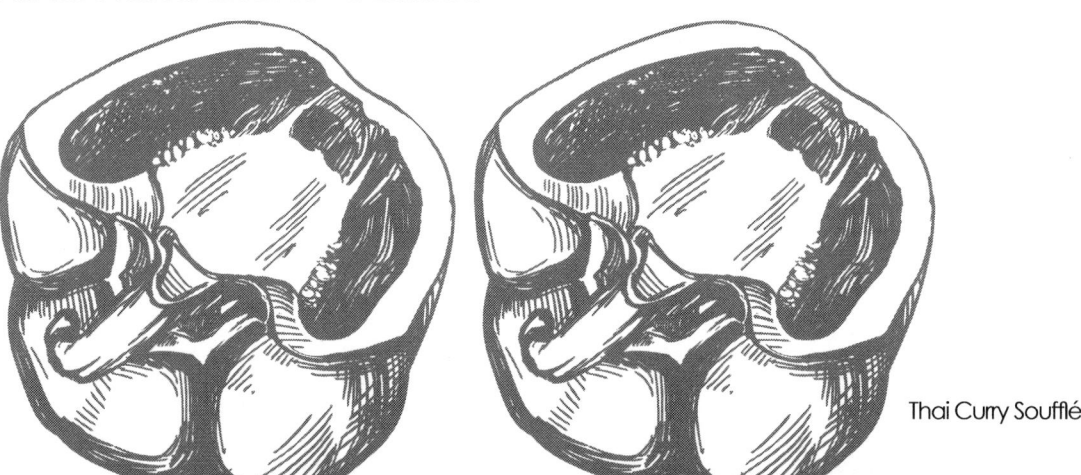

Pecan Soufflé

Prep Time: 45 mins
Total Time: 1 hr 45 mins

Servings per Recipe: 4
Calories   299.8
Fat   12.5g
Cholesterol   74.1mg
Sodium   317.0mg
Carbohydrates   45.2g
Protein   3.9g

Ingredients

1 3/4 lb. carrots, with tops
6 tbsp butter, softened
3/4 C. sugar
1/2 C. all-purpose flour
1 1/2 tsp baking powder
1/2 tsp vanilla extract
1/2 tsp salt

3 eggs
Topping:
1/2 C. grated carrot
1/2 C. chopped pecans
3/4 C. light brown sugar

Directions

1. Remove the tops from the carrots and refrigerate before using.
2. Peel the carrots and cut into chunks.
3. In a 3-quart pan, place carrots and enough water to cover and bring to a boil.
4. Reduce the heat to medium and cook, covered for about 20 minutes.
5. Drain the carrots well and keep aside t cool slightly.
6. Set your oven to 350 degrees F and grease a 2-quart casserole dish.
7. In a food processor, add the carrots, eggs, butter, flour, sugar, baking powder, vanilla and salt and pulse until pureed.
8. For the pecan topping: in a bowl, mix together the grated carrots, brown sugar and pecans.
9. Place the pureed mixture into the prepared casserole dish and sprinkle with the topping mixture evenly.
10. Cook in the oven for about 55-65 minutes.
11. Remove from the oven and invert the soufflé onto a serving platter.
12. Serve warm.

HONEY
Butter Soufflé

Prep Time: 20 mins
Total Time: 32 mins

Servings per Recipe: 2
Calories	188.3
Fat	5.5g
Cholesterol	100.6mg
Sodium	141.9mg
Carbohydrates	27.6g
Protein	6.1g

Ingredients

1 large egg
1 egg white
1/4 C. almond milk, slightly warmed
1/4 C. sweet rice flour
1 pinch salt
2 tsp honey
1/2 tsp vanilla
1/2 tbsp clarified butter

1/2 C. fruit
2 tsp maple syrup
1/4 C. berries
1 tsp organic powdered sugar

Directions

1. Set your oven to 450 degrees F before doing anything else.
2. In a small bowl, add the egg white and beat until soft peaks form.
3. In another bowl, add the whole egg and sweet rice flour and beat until well combined.
4. Add the salt, honey and vanilla and beat until well combined.
5. Add the warm milk and stir to combine.
6. Gently, fold the whipped eggs whites into the flour mixture.
7. In a 6-inch oven-proof skillet, melt the coconut oil over medium-low heat and tilt the pan to spread evenly.
8. Place the mixture in small amounts and cook for about 2-3 minutes.
9. Sprinkle some fruit on top of the pancake and transfer the pan into the oven.
10. Cook in the oven for about 7-8 minutes.
11. Remove from the oven and drizzle with the maple syrup.
12. Top with he extra fruit and serve with a sprinkling of the powdered sugar.

Alternative Leek Soufflé

Prep Time: 30 mins
Total Time: 1 hr

Servings per Recipe: 4
Calories	445.9
Fat	30.7g
Cholesterol	254.7mg
Sodium	848.0mg
Carbohydrates	22.9g
Protein	19.4g

Ingredients

- 1/2 C. packaged breadcrumbs
- 60 g butter
- 1 medium leek, finely chopped
- 1/4 C. plain flour
- 1 C. milk
- 1 tsp grainy mustard
- 150 g Stilton cheese, crumbled
- 4 eggs, separated

Directions

1. Set your oven to 350 degrees F before doing anything else and lightly, grease 4 oven-proof soufflé bowls. Then, sprinkle with the breadcrumbs, shaking off the excess crumbs.
2. In a pan, melt the butter and sauté the leek until soft.
3. Stir in the flour over low heat and cook until bubbling, stirring continuously.
4. Remove the pan from heat and slowly, stir in the milk, stirring continuously until well combined.
5. Return the pan to heat and bring to a boil, stirring continuously.
6. Transfer the mixture into a large bowl.
7. Add the mustard, cheese and egg yolks and stir until well combined.
8. In a small bowl, add the egg whites and beat until soft peaks form.
9. In two portions, gently fold the whipped egg whites into the yolk mixture.
10. Place the mixture into the prepared bowls evenly.
11. Arrange the bowls onto a baking sheet.
12. Cook in the oven for about 15 minutes.

5-INGREDIENT
Corn Soufflé

🥣 Prep Time: 10 mins
🕐 Total Time: 1 hr 10 mins

Servings per Recipe: 8
Calories 376.7
Fat 19.3g
Cholesterol 158.2mg
Sodium 1091.7mg
Carbohydrates 36.9g
Protein 18.5g

Ingredients

3 (15 oz.) cans creamed corn
5 large eggs (slightly beaten)
1/2 C. half-and-half
16 oz. of shredded cheese
salt and pepper

Directions

1. Set your oven to 350 degrees F before doing anything else.
2. In a large casserole dish, place the creamed corn.
3. Add the cheese, eggs, half-and-half, salt and pepper and beat until well combined.
4. Cook in the oven for about 1 hour.

Pistachios Soufflé

Prep Time: 50 mins
Total Time: 4 hrs 50 mins

Servings per Recipe: 8
Calories   288.6
Fat   19.7g
Cholesterol   202.8mg
Sodium   59.1mg
Carbohydrates   23.2g
Protein   6.0g

Ingredients

10 -16 oz. tangerines, fresh (1 tsp fresh tangerine zest, and 1/2 C. juice)
1 (1/4 oz.) envelope unflavored gelatin
1/4 tsp vanilla extract
6 egg yolks, at room temperature
2/3 C. granulated sugar
5 egg whites, chilled
12 oz. heavy cream (whipping cream)
1/3 C. pistachios, chopped (optional)

Directions

1. For a collar: cut a sheet of the waxed paper that's long enough to fit around a 1-quart soufflé dish.
2. Fold in the quarters lengthwise to make a ribbon about 3-inch wide.
3. Wrap the collar around the top of the soufflé dish and secure the ends together with the tape.
4. Freeze the pan to chill.
5. In a small pan, mix together the tangerine zest and juice over low heat.
6. Add the gelatin and stir until dissolved.
7. Add the vanilla extract and stir to combine.
8. Remove the pan from the heat and place in a large bowl of the ice water until the mixture thickens into a jelly.
9. Bring a small stockpot of water to a simmer. Mix egg yolks & sugar
10. In a medium glass mixing bowl, mix together the egg yolks and sugar.
11. Arrange the bowl of sugar mixture over the pan of a simmering water and cook until mixture becomes pale, beating continuously.
12. Remove from the heat and add the cooled tangerine mixture, beating continuously until cooled, thick and sticky.

13. In a medium bowl, add the egg whites and beat until stiff peaks form.
14. Refrigerate before using.
15. In another large bowl, add the heavy cream and beat until soft peaks form.
16. Place half of the egg whites into the cooled egg yolk mixture and stir until its color becomes lighter.
17. Add the remaining egg whites into the large bowl of whipped cream and top with the tangerine mixture.
18. Gently fold all the mixtures together.
19. Transfer the mixture into the chilled soufflé dish about halfway up the paper collar.
20. Freeze for about 4 hours.
21. Just before serving, sprinkle with the pistachios and carefully remove the collar.
22. With a very sharp knife, cut into desired sized sections and serve.

Caster Espresso Soufflé

Prep Time: 35 mins
Total Time: 45 mins

Servings per Recipe: 4
Calories 174.0
Fat 8.9g
Cholesterol 102.5mg
Sodium 99.3mg
Carbohydrates 19.6g
Protein 4.1g

Ingredients

- 1/2 C. milk
- 1/4 C. espresso coffee
- 3 1/2 tbsp caster sugar
- 2 tbsp butter
- 2 tbsp cornstarch
- 2 egg yolks
- 2 egg whites
- 1 tbsp caster sugar, extra

Directions

1. Set your oven to 350 degrees F before doing anything else and arrange an oven tray in the oven to heat.
2. Grease the moulds and sprinkle each with the sugar, shaking off the excess.
3. For the custard: in a small pan, add the milk, sugar and coffee and bring to a boil, stir continuously Remove from the heat and keep aside.
4. In another pan, melt the butter over a gentle heat and add the cornflour, beating continuously until smooth.
5. Add the milk mixture, beating continuously until the mixture becomes thick.
6. Remove from the heat and keep aside to cool slightly.
7. Add the egg yolks and stir vigorously until a glossy mixture is formed.
8. Keep aside to cool completely. In a bowl, add the egg whites and beat until soft peak form. Add the extra tbsp of the caster sugar and beat until glossy.
9. Add about 1/4 of the egg white mixture into the cooled custard and stir to combine well.
10. Gently, fold in the remaining egg whites mixture.
11. Transfer the mixture into the prepared moulds about 3/4 of full.
12. With your finger, create an indentation between the the filling.
13. Arrange the moulds onto the hot oven tray and cook in the oven for about 10 minutes.

LEMONY Applesauce Soufflé

Prep Time: 10 mins
Total Time: 45 mins

Servings per Recipe: 4
Calories   179.4
Fat   4.1g
Cholesterol   159.8mg
Sodium   288.6mg
Carbohydrates   26.5g
Protein   9.3g

Ingredients

150 g mixed berries
3 eggs, separated
1 C. Splenda sugar substitute
1 C. skim milk
1/2 C. self-raising flour, sifted
1/4 C. lemon juice

30 g sugar-free applesauce
2 tsp grated lemon rind (optional)
water, boiled

Directions

1. Set your oven to 350 degrees F before doing anything else and grease 3 (1-C.) soufflé dishes.
2. In a bowl, add the egg yolks and half of the Splenda and with an electric mixer, beat until thick and creamy.
3. Add the flour, applesauce, skim milk, lemon juice and lemon rind and stir to combine.
4. In another large bowl, add the egg whites and beat until soft peaks form.
5. Slowly, add the remaining Splenda, beating continuously until thick and glossy.
6. Gently, fold egg yolk mixture into the egg whites.
7. Divide the mixed berries into the prepared dishes evenly and top with the egg mixture.
8. Arrange the dishes in a large baking pan and add enough hot water to come halfway up sides of the dishes.
9. Cook in the oven for about 35-40 minutes.

Matzo American Soufflé

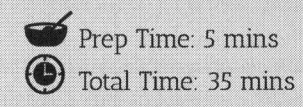

Prep Time: 5 mins
Total Time: 35 mins

Servings per Recipe: 6
Calories   222.0
Fat   12.5g
Cholesterol   91.9mg
Sodium   409.7mg
Carbohydrates   15.0g
Protein   12.0g

Ingredients

butter, for the pan
5 matzos
water
1 (10 1/2 oz.) cans tomato sauce & mushrooms
onion powder (optional)
garlic powder (optional)
1/2-3/4 lb. American cheese, sliced
2 large eggs
1 C. milk

Directions

1. Set your oven to 375 degrees F before doing anything else and lightly, grease a 13x9-inch baking dish.
2. In a bowl, add the eggs and milk and beat until well combined.
3. With water, wet the matzos lightly.
4. In the bottom of the prepared baking dish, arrange 2 1/2 matzos.
5. Place half of the tomato sauce over the matzos and top with the cheese slices, followed by the remaining matzos and remaining sauce.
6. Sprinkle with the onion and garlic powder and top with the egg mixture.
7. Cook in the oven for about 30 minutes.
8. Remove from the oven and keep aside for about 10 minutes before serving.

4-INGREDIENT
Soufflé

🥣 Prep Time: 15 mins
🕒 Total Time: 55 mins

Servings per Recipe: 12
Calories	254.7
Fat	15.2g
Cholesterol	105.9mg
Sodium	561.0mg
Carbohydrates	15.9g
Protein	13.3g

Ingredients

50 saltine crackers
4 C. cheese, grated
4 -5 eggs
4 C. milk

Directions

1. Grease a 13x9-inch baking dish.
2. In a bowl, add the eggs and milk and beat well.
3. In the bottom of the prepared baking dish, arrange a layer of the crackers ad top with a layer of cheese.
4. Repeat the layers, ending with the cheese.
5. top with the egg mixture evenly and keep aside for at least about 30 minutes.
6. Set your oven to 350 degrees F.
7. Cook in the oven for about 40 minutes.
8. Remove from the oven and serve.

Deep Vanilla Soufflé

Prep Time: 50 mins
Total Time: 1 hr 15 mins

Servings per Recipe: 4
Calories   1031.8
Fat   71.0g
Cholesterol   791.8mg
Sodium   210.7mg
Carbohydrates   82.1g
Protein   15.6g

Ingredients

granulated sugar
3 tbsp butter
3 tbsp all-purpose flour
3/4 C. half-and-half
6 tbsp granulated sugar, divided
4 large eggs, separated
2 tbsp vanilla extract
sifted powdered sugar

1 tsp vanilla extract
1 C. sugar
2 tsp cornstarch
2 C. whipping cream
8 egg yolks

Directions

1. Set your oven to 350 degrees F before doing anything else and grease 4 (6-oz.) baking dishes and sprinkle with the granulated sugar.
2. In a small pan, melt the butter over medium heat and add the flour, stirring until smooth.
3. Cook for about minute, stirring continuously.
4. Slowly, add the half-and-half, stirring continuously until well combined.
5. Stir in 4 tbsp of the and cook until thick, stirring continuously.
6. Remove from the heat.
7. In a bowl, add the egg yolks and beat until thick and pale.
8. Slowly, add half of the hot half-and-half mixture and stir to combine.
9. stir in the remaining hot mixture and cook over medium heat for about 2 minutes.
10. Stir in the vanilla and keep aside to cool for about 15-20 minutes.
11. In another bowl, add the egg whites and with an electric mixer, beat on high speed until foamy.
12. Slowly, add the remaining 2 tbsp of the sugar, beating until soft peaks form.
13. Gently, fold egg whites into the egg yolk mixture.

14. Transfer the mixture into the prepared baking dishes evenly.
15. Cook in the oven for about 25 minutes.
16. Meanwhile, for the vanilla crème sauce: in a heavy pan, add 1 tsp of the vanilla extract, 1 C. of the sugar and 2 tsp of the cornstarch.
17. Stir in the whipping cream and cook over low heat until sugar is dissolved, stirring continuously.
18. In a bowl, add 8 egg yolks and beat until thick and pale.
19. Slowly, stir about half of hot whipping cream mixture into yolks.
20. Add the remaining hot mixture, stirring continuously.
21. Cook over medium heat until thickened, stirring continuously.
22. Through a wire-mesh strainer, strain the mixture into a small bowl,.
23. Refrigerate, covered before serving.
24. remove from the oven and sprinkle with the powdered sugar.
25. Serve immediately alongside the vanilla crème sauce.

2-Cheese Fruity Soufflé

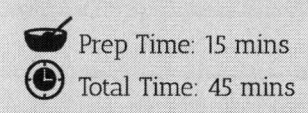

Prep Time: 15 mins
Total Time: 45 mins

Servings per Recipe: 2
Calories	636.1
Fat	47.6g
Cholesterol	481.1mg
Sodium	1177.5mg
Carbohydrates	17.6g
Protein	33.7g

Ingredients

- 3 tbsp unsalted butter
- 1/4 C. finely grated fresh Parmesan cheese
- 3 tbsp all-purpose flour
- 1 C. scalded milk
- kosher salt
- fresh ground black pepper
- 1 pinch cayenne pepper
- 1 pinch nutmeg
- 4 extra-large egg yolks, at room temperature
- 3 oz. good Roquefort cheese, chopped
- 5 extra large egg whites, at room temperature
- 1/8 tsp cream of tartar

Topping:
- fresh fruit or frozen fruit

Directions

1. Set your oven to 400 degrees F before doing anything else and arrange a rack in the middle of the oven.
2. Grease a 7 1/2x3 1/4-inch soufflé dish with some butter and sprinkle with the Parmesan cheese.
3. In a small pan, melt the butter over low heat and stir in the flour.
4. Cook for about 2 minutes, stirring continuously.
5. Remove from the heat and add the hot milk, nutmeg, cayenne, 1/2 tsp of the salt and 1/4 tsp of the black pepper, beating continuously.
6. Place the pan over low heat and cook for about 1 minute, beating continuously.
7. Remove from the heat and add the egg yolks, one at a time, beating continuously.
8. Add the Roquefort and 1/4 C. of the Parmesan cheese and stir to combine.
9. Transfer the mixture into a large bowl.
10. In the bowl of an electric mixer, fitted with the whisk attachment, add the egg whites, cream of tartar and a pinch of salt and beat on low speed for about 1 minute.

11. Now, beat on medium speed for about 1 minute and finally, beat on high speed until firm and glossy peaks are formed.
12. Add about 1/4 of the egg whites into the cheese sauce and beat until well combined.
13. Then, fold in the remaining egg whites.
14. Transfer the mixture into the prepared soufflé dish and with the back of a spoon, smooth the top.
15. With the spatula, draw a circle on top of the soufflé.
16. Arrange the soufflé dish in the oven and set it to 375 degrees F.
17. Cook in the oven for about 30-35 minutes.
18. Remove from the oven and serve immediately with the topping of fruit.

Denver Soufflé

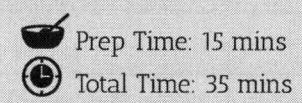

Prep Time: 15 mins
Total Time: 35 mins

Servings per Recipe: 6
Calories	264.5
Fat	251.4mg
Cholesterol	930.4mg
Sodium	6.5g
Carbohydrates	15.8g
Protein	264.5

Ingredients

- 2 tbsp butter
- 2 C. sliced mushrooms
- 6 -10 eggs, separated
- 1 tsp salt
- 1 tsp pepper
- 1 tsp baking powder
- 1 C. milk
- 2 C. cheese, grated

Directions

1. Heat a large electric frying pan to 300 degrees F.
2. Add the butter and fry the mushrooms until tender.
3. In a bowl, add the egg whites and beat until stiff.
4. In another bowl, add the milk, egg yolks, flour, baking powder, salt and pepper and beat until well combined.
5. Fold the egg whites into the yolk mixture.
6. Gently, place the egg mixture over the mushrooms.
7. With a lid, seal the skillet tightly and cook for about 10-15 minutes.
8. Uncover and sprinkle with the cheese evenly.
9. Again, close the lid and cook for about 5 minutes more.
10. Cut into squares and serve.

2-PINEAPPLE Soufflé

Prep Time: 20 mins
Total Time: 20 mins

Servings per Recipe: 8
Calories   308.2
Fat   7.7g
Cholesterol   25.1mg
Sodium   289.7mg
Carbohydrates   56.8g
Protein   5.7g

Ingredients

100 g cream cheese
1 can sliced pineapple
1 (85 g) packages pineapple Jell-O
2 C. whipped cream, sweetened

Directions

1. For the Jell-O, in a bowl, dissolve the packet into 1 1/2 C. of boiling water.
2. Refrigerate until set.
3. In a blender, add 5 slices pineapple slices, whipped cream, cream cheese and Jell-O and pulse until pureed.
4. Transfer into the bowl and refrigerate for about 8 hours.
5. Chop the remaining pineapple slices roughly.
6. Serve the soufflé with the topping of chopped pineapple slices.

Authentic Vegan Soufflé

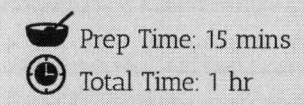

Prep Time: 15 mins
Total Time: 1 hr

Servings per Recipe: 12
Calories 363.8
Fat 14.8g
Cholesterol 0.0mg
Sodium 153.1mg
Carbohydrates 55.7g
Protein 3.9g

Ingredients

Filling:
- 5 -6 medium sweet potatoes, baked, peeled and mashed
- 1 (8 oz.) packages firm silken tofu
- 8 oz. tofutti better-than-cream-cheese
- 1 C. brown sugar
- 2 tbsp soy margarine, melted
- 1 tbsp cornstarch
- 2 tbsp pumpkin pie spice
- 1 tbsp pure vanilla extract

Garnish:
- 3/4 C. flour
- 1 C. brown sugar
- 6 tbsp soy margarine
- 1 C. pecans, chopped

Directions

1. Set your oven to 350 degrees F before doing anything else and grease an 8x13-inch baking dish.
2. In a food processor, add the sweet potatoes and silken tofu and pulse until smooth.
3. Add the remaining filling ingredients and pulse until smooth.
4. For topping, in another bowl, mix together the flour and brown sugar.
5. With a pastry blender, cut in the soy margarine until a crumbly mixture is formed.
6. Add the pecans and stir to combine.
7. Transfer the filling into an 8x13-inch greased baking dish and top with the topping mixture evenly.
8. Cook in the oven for about 35-45 minutes.

BURRITO Soufflé

Prep Time: 10 mins
Total Time: 15 mins

Servings per Recipe: 2
Calories   308.6
Fat   18.1g
Cholesterol   126.0mg
Sodium   616.0mg
Carbohydrates   21.8g
Protein   14.8g

Ingredients

1 C. broccoli, frozen
1 egg
1 egg white
2 tbsp milk
2 oz. cheese
2 flour tortillas
1 tbsp margarine
salt
pepper

Directions

1. In a microwave-safe bowl, add the broccoli with a little water and microwave for about 6 minutes.
2. Drain the broccoli well and keep aside.
3. Meanwhile, in a bowl, add the milk, egg, egg white, salt and pepper and beat until frothy.
4. In a frying pan, melt the margarine and cook the egg mixture until desired doneness, stirring continuously.
5. Transfer the scrambled eggs into a bowl with the broccoli and mix.
6. In a microwave-safe place, place the tortillas and microwave for about 1 minute.
7. Arrange the tortillas onto a smooth surface.
8. Place the broccoli mixture in the middle of each tortilla and top each with a cheese slice.
9. Roll each tortilla like a burrito and tuck the ends in and roll, enveloping entire mixture inside.
10. Place the burritos in the warm skillet, flap-side down and cook until the cheese is melted.
11. Flip and coo until heated from other side.
12. Serve warm.

Chicken & Mushroom Soufflé

 Prep Time: 20 mins
 Total Time: 1 hr 35 mins

Servings per Recipe: 6
Calories   483.7
Fat   22.7g
Cholesterol   236.3mg
Sodium   1858.2mg
Carbohydrates   29.0g
Protein   38.9g

Ingredients

9 slices bread, cut into cubes
4 C. diced cooked chicken
1 (4 oz.) cans mushrooms, drained
1 C. diced celery
1/4 C. diced onion
2 tbsp lemon juice
1/2 C. Miracle Whip
1 C. grated cheddar cheese
4 eggs, beaten

2 C. chicken broth
1 (10 3/4 oz.) cans cream of celery soup
1 tsp salt
1/4 tsp pepper
1 (10 3/4 oz.) cans cream of mushroom soup
buttered breadcrumbs

Directions

1. In a bowl, add the chicken, mushrooms, onion, celery, lemon juice and miracle whip and mix until well combined.
2. In another bowl, add the eggs, celery, cream of celery soup, broth, salt and pepper and beat until well combined.
3. In the bottom of a greased 10x14-inch baking dish, spread about 2/3 of the breadcrumbs.
4. Place the chicken mixture over breadcrumbs, followed by the remaining 1/3 of breadcrumbs, cheese and egg mixture evenly.
5. Refrigerate overnight.
6. Remove from the refrigerator and top with the the cream of mushroom soup evenly.
7. Keep the baking dish aside until it reaches room temperature.
8. Set your oven to 350 degrees F.
9. Cook in the oven for about 1 hour.
10. Remove from the oven and top with the buttered breadcrumbs evenly.
11. Cook in the oven for about 15 minutes more.

SCALLION Soufflé

Prep Time: 20 mins
Total Time: 50 mins

Servings per Recipe: 6
Calories   518.0
Fat   38.3g
Cholesterol   353.7mg
Sodium   639.9mg
Carbohydrates   9.9g
Protein   32.8g

Ingredients

7 large eggs, separated, whites at room temperature
1 1/2 C. milk
1/2 C. thinly-sliced scallion, including green part
6 tbsp all-purpose flour
3 tbsp butter
1 lb. grated Gruyere cheese
1/2 tsp baking soda
1/2 tsp baking powder
1/4 tsp salt

Directions

1. In a bowl, add the milk and egg yolks and beat until well combined.
2. In another bowl, add the flour and add the milk mixture in a very slow stream, beating continuously well combined.
3. In a large skillet, melt the butter over medium-low heat and cook the leeks until tender, stirring continuously. Increase the heat to medium.
4. Stir in the custard mixture and bring to a gentle boil, beating continuously.
5. Add the Gruyere and cook until the cheese is just melted.
6. Transfer the mixture into a large bowl and season with the salt.
7. Set your oven to 350 degrees F before doing anything else and arrange a rack in upper third of the oven. Grease a a 13x9-inch Pyrex baking dish.
8. In a bowl, add the egg whites, baking soda, baking powder and salt and beat until they hold stiff peaks. Gently, fold 1/3 of white mixture into the cheese mixture.
9. Then, gently fold in the remaining white mixture.
10. Place the mixture into the prepared baking dish evenly.
11. Cook in the oven for about 25-30 minutes.
12. Remove from the oven and serve immediately.

Lemon Soufflé

Prep Time: 20 mins
Total Time: 1 hr 20 mins

Servings per Recipe: 4
Calories	973.7
Fat	57.1g
Cholesterol	476.8mg
Sodium	642.3mg
Carbohydrates	102.4g
Protein	17.2g

Ingredients

- 1/2 C. butter, at room temperature
- 1 1/2 C. sugar
- 6 large eggs, separated, whites at room temperature
- 2/3 C. lemon juice
- 2/3 C. all-purpose flour
- 3 lemons, zest of, grated
- 2 C. milk
- 1 C. heavy cream
- 1/2 tsp salt

Directions

1. Set your oven to 350 degrees F before doing anything else and lightly, grease a 9x2-inch round cake pan.
2. In a bowl, add the butter and sugar and beat until creamy.
3. Slowly, add the egg yolks, one at a time and beat until well combined.
4. Add the lemon juice, flour and zest and stir to combine well.
5. Add the milk and cream and stir to combine.
6. In another bowl, add the egg whites and salt and beat until stiff peaks form.
7. Add 1/4 of the white mixture into the lemon mixture and stir to combine.
8. Then, fold in remaining whites.
9. Transfer the mixture into the prepared cake pan.
10. Arrange the cake pan in a large roasting pan and add enough hot water to come halfway up sides.
11. Cook in the oven for about 50-60 minutes.
12. Remove from the oven and serve warm.

NOODLES
& Spinach Soufflé

Prep Time: 10 mins
Total Time: 55 mins

Servings per Recipe: 4
Calories 621.1
Fat 36.5g
Cholesterol 208.2mg
Sodium 728.8mg
Carbohydrates 48.5g
Protein 24.8g

Ingredients

1 (12 oz.) packages Bouffer spinach Soufflé, thawed
8 oz. freshly cooked extra wide egg noodles
1 C. sour cream
2 tbsp pesto sauce
1/4 tsp nutmeg
1 C. extra-sharp cheddar cheese, grated

Directions

1. Set your oven to 350 degrees F before doing anything else and grease an 8x8x2-inch baking dish.
2. In a bowl, add all the ingredients except the cheese and mix until well combined.
3. Place the mixture into the prepared baking dish and top with the cheese evenly.
4. Cook in the oven for about 45 minutes.
5. Remove from the oven and keep aside for about 10 minutes before serving.

Cheese & Bread Soufflé

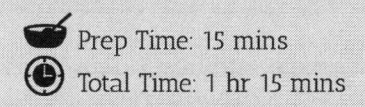

Prep Time: 15 mins
Total Time: 1 hr 15 mins

Servings per Recipe: 6
Calories   355.8
Fat   20.6g
Cholesterol   194.7mg
Sodium   751.2mg
Carbohydrates   22.4g
Protein   19.5g

Ingredients

8 slices bread, cut into 1/2 inch squares
2 1/2 C. milk
4 eggs
1/2 tsp dry mustard
1/2 tsp salt
pepper
2 C. sharp cheddar cheese, grated
1 can diced Chile, rinsed and drained

Directions

1. In the bottom of an 8x12-inch baking dish, arrange the bread squares.
2. In a large bowl, add the eggs, milk, mustard, salt and pepper and beat until well combined.
3. Stir in the cheese and chilies.
4. Place the milk mixture over the bread and toss to moisten.
5. Refrigerate, covered at least 8 hours or overnight.
6. Set your oven to 325 degrees F.
7. Uncover and cook in the oven for about 1 hour.
8. Remove from the oven and serve immediately.

PHYLLO CUPS
Soufflé

Prep Time: 20 mins
Total Time: 50 mins

Servings per Recipe: 8
Calories   319.4
Fat   26.3g
Cholesterol   94.6mg
Sodium   347.9mg
Carbohydrates   12.1g
Protein   9.1g

Ingredients

Cups:
6 (17x12-inch) phyllo pastry sheets, thawed if frozen
1/4 C. unsalted butter, melted
Filling:
2 tbsp unsalted butter
2 tbsp all-purpose flour
3/4 C. whole milk
2 tsp Dijon mustard
2 large eggs, separated
1 oz. finely grated parmigiano-reggiano cheese
5 oz. soft mild goat cheese, crumbled
Salad:
1 1/2 tbsp cider vinegar
1 1/2 tsp Dijon mustard
1/4 tsp salt
5 tbsp extra virgin olive oil
8 oz. frisee, torn into bite-size pieces
6 radishes, cut into very thin wedges
3 tbsp chopped fresh chives

Directions

1. Set your oven to 375 degrees F before doing anything else and arrange a rack in the middle of oven.
2. With 2 overlapping plastic wrap sheets and a dampened kitchen towel, cover the phyllo stack.
3. Coat 6 phyllo sheets with some melted butter.
4. Arrange 1 phyllo sheet onto a smooth surface and top with remaining 2 buttered sheets.
5. repeat with remaining 3 sheets.
6. With a sharp knife, cut each buttwered stack into 6 (4 1/2-inch) squares and trim the excess sides.
7. Arrange 1 square in each of 8 muffin cups.
8. Cook the phyllo cups in the oven for about 8 minutes.
9. Remove from the oven and keep aside onto a wire rack to cool completely in the pan.

10. Now, set your oven to 400 degrees F and arrange a rack in the middle of oven.
11. For the filling: in a 3-quart heavy pan, melt the butter over medium-low heat and add the flour, beating continuously.
12. Cook for about 3 minutes, beating continuously.
13. Slowly, Stir in the milk and bring to a boil, beating continuously.
14. Reduce the heat and simmer for about 5 minutes, beating occasionally.
15. Remove from the heat and add the egg yolks, mustard and 1/4 C. of the Parmigiano-Reggiano, beating continuously until well combined.
16. Gently, fold in the goat cheese.
17. In a large bowl, add the egg whites and with an electric mixer, beat until they just hold stiff peaks.
18. Fold 1/3 of the whites into sauce.
19. Then, gently fold in the remaining whites.
20. Place the filling mixture into 8 phyllo cups and sprinkle with the remaining Parmigiano-Reggiano.
21. Cook in the oven for about 15 minutes.
22. Remove from the oven and keep aside to cool slightly.
23. For the dressing: in a bowl, add the mustard, vinegar and salt and beat well.
24. Slowly, add oil in a slow stream and beat until smooth.
25. For the salad: in a large bowl, add the frisée, radishes and dressing and toss to coat.
26. Divide salad onto 8 plates and sprinkle with the chives.
27. Arrange 1 soufflé cup over each plate and serve immediately

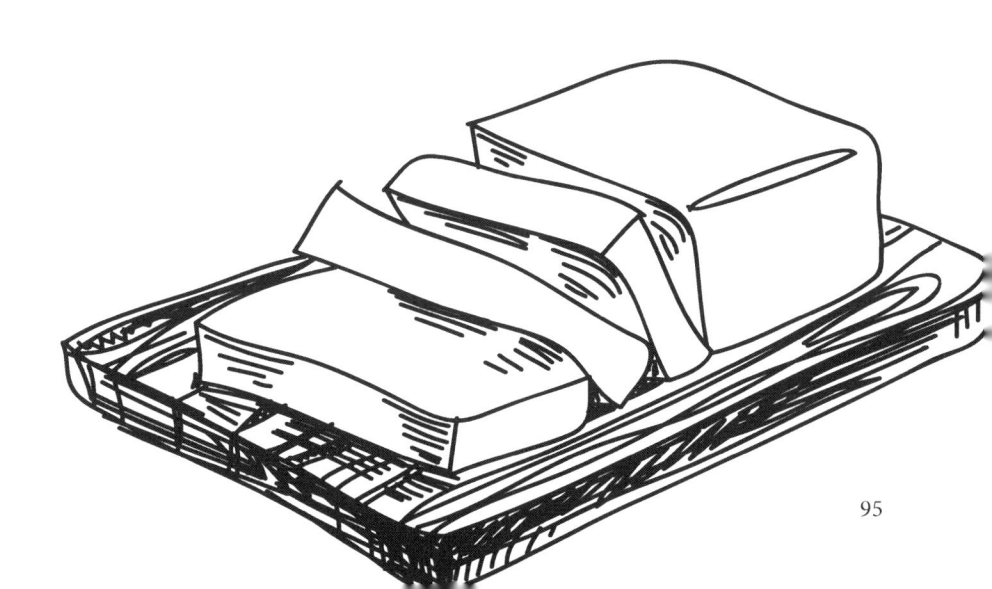

CHEDDAR
Soufflé

🥣 Prep Time: 15 mins
🕐 Total Time: 25 mins

Servings per Recipe: 4
Calories 143.2
Fat 5.9g
Cholesterol 212.2mg
Sodium 242.7mg
Carbohydrates 13.2g
Protein 8.3g

Ingredients

4 slices bread, crusts removed
4 oz. white cheddar cheese, sliced
4 eggs, separated
4 tsp milk
salt and pepper

Directions

1. Set your oven to 350 degrees F before doing anything else and lightly, grease a baking dish.
2. Toast each bread slices on one side.
3. In a bowl, add the milk, egg yolks, salt and pepper and beat until well combined.
4. In another bowl, add the egg whites and beat until very stiff.
5. Gently, fold egg yolks into the whipped egg whites.
6. Arrange the bread slices in the prepared baking dish, toasted side down.
7. place the cheese slices over the bread slices and top with the egg mixture.
8. Cook in the oven for about 10-15 minutes.
9. Remove from the oven and serve immediately.

Spiced Soufflé

Prep Time: 10 mins
Total Time: 50 mins

Servings per Recipe: 6
Calories	310.6
Fat	20.4g
Cholesterol	161.4mg
Sodium	777.3mg
Carbohydrates	15.8g
Protein	16.3g

Ingredients

- 2 (4 oz.) cans green chilies, chopped
- 1/2 lb. sharp cheddar cheese, shredded
- 3/4 C. dry breadcrumbs
- 3 eggs
- 1 tsp parsley flakes
- 1/2 tsp ground cumin
- 1 tsp salt
- 1 tsp oregano
- 1/2 C. light cream
- 1/2 C. milk

Directions

1. Set your oven to 375 degrees F before doing anything else and grease a 13x9-inch glass baking dish.
2. In a bowl, add the eggs and beat until light and fluffy.
3. Add the milk, cream, parsley flakes, cumin, oregano and salt and beat until well combined.
4. In the bottom of prepared baking dish, arrange the chilies and top with the cheese, followed by breadcrumbs and egg mixture.
5. Cook in the oven for about 40 minutes.

TANGERINE
Soufflé

🥣 Prep Time: 5 mins
🕐 Total Time: 16 mins

Servings per Recipe: 4
Calories	305.7
Fat	16.1g
Cholesterol	5.0mg
Sodium	125.1mg
Carbohydrates	39.2g
Protein	3.2g

Ingredients

2 tangerines
1 (3 oz.) boxes lemon gelatin
1/2 C. water, boiling (plus a little for the juice)
1 (8 oz.) containers frozen whipped topping, thawed
1/4 C. light sour cream

Directions

1. Grate the zest of 1 tangerine and them squeeze its juice in a small bowl.
2. Add Enough water to measure about 1/2 C. of the juice mixture.
3. Peel the remaining tangerine and then, divide into sections.
4. In a bowl, dissolve the gelatin into 1/2 C. of boiling water.
5. Arrange the bowl of gelatin mixture in an ice bath for 2 minutes.
6. Then, fold in the frozen whipped topping and sour cream.
7. Divide tangerine segments and cream mixture into 4 (6-oz.) ramekins with 2-inch wax-paper collars.
8. Refrigerate for about 5 minutes before serving.

Sausage Soufflé

🥘 Prep Time: 20 mins
🕐 Total Time: 1 hr 5 mins

Servings per Recipe: 8
Calories   453.6
Fat   29.8g
Cholesterol   158.3mg
Sodium   847.8mg
Carbohydrates   22.3g
Protein   22.8g

Ingredients

12 slices white bread, cut into 1 inch cubes
1 lb. sausage links
2 C. cheddar cheese, shredded
3 eggs, beaten
2 C. milk
1/2 tsp dry mustard
salt and pepper

Directions

1. Set the broiler of your oven.
2. Cook the sausage under the broiler until browned.
3. Transfer the sausage onto a paper towel-lined plate to drain.
4. Grease a 13x9-inch baking dish.
5. In a bowl, add the milk, eggs, dry mustard, salt and pepper and beat until well combined.
6. In the bottom of the prepared baking dish, arrange half of the bred cubes and top with half of the cheese, remaining bread cubes, egg mixture, remaining cheese and cooked sausage.
7. Refrigerate overnight.
8. Now, set your oven to 350 degrees F.
9. Cook in the oven for about 45 minutes.

CRAB & Coconut Soufflé

Prep Time: 30 mins
Total Time: 1 hr 5 mins

Servings per Recipe: 8
Calories 176.5
Fat 11.5g
Cholesterol 115.5mg
Sodium 465.2mg
Carbohydrates 7.2g
Protein 10.9g

Ingredients

1/2 C. sweetened flaked coconut
4 tbsp unsalted butter
1/3 C. celery top
1 garlic clove, minced
1/2 tsp curry powder
1/2 tsp dried thyme
1/2 tsp red pepper flakes
1/2 tsp salt
ground black pepper

3 tbsp unbleached all-purpose flour
1 1/4 C. milk
4 egg yolks
1/2 lb. crab meat
6 egg whites, stiffly beaten
1/4 tsp fresh lemon juice

Directions

1. Set your oven to 400 degrees F before doing anything else and arrange a rack in the bottom of the oven. Grease an 8 C. soufflé dish.
2. Heat a non-stick skillet over low heat and cook the coconut until toasted.
3. In a medium skillet, melt the butter over low heat and cook the celery, garlic, thyme, curry powder, red pepper flakes, salt and pepper for about 3 minutes.
4. Stir in the flour and cook for about 1 minute, stirring continuously.
5. Increase the heat to medium. Stir in the milk and cook until mixture becomes thick, stirring continuously. Remove from the heat and keep aside to cool slightly.
6. In the sauce, add the egg yolks, one at a time and beat until well combined.
7. Stir in the crab meat and coconut. In a bowl, add the egg whites and lemon juice and with a mixer, beat until stiff, but not dry. Add 1/4 of the egg whites into the crab mixture and stir to combine. Gently, fold in the remaining whites.
8. Transfer the mixture into the prepared soufflé dish.
9. Cook in the oven for about 30 minutes.
10. Remove from the oven and serve immediately.

Cheesy Herb Soufflé

Prep Time: 20 mins
Total Time: 1 hr 5 mins

Servings per Recipe: 1
Calories   2568.7
Fat   199.5g
Cholesterol   2162.7mg
Sodium   4925.3mg
Carbohydrates   65.0g
Protein   128.0g

Ingredients

- 2 C. milk
- 6 tbsp butter
- 6 tbsp all-purpose flour
- 8 eggs, separated
- 1 C. grated Monterey Jack cheese
- 1 C. grated cheddar cheese
- 1 tsp Grey Poupon mustard
- 2 tbsp fresh basil, finely chopped
- 2 tbsp fresh rosemary, finely chopped
- 2 tbsp fresh thyme, finely chopped
- 1/2 tsp nutmeg
- 1 tsp salt
- pepper

Directions

1. Set your oven to 350 degrees F before doing anything else and generously, grease a soufflé dish.
2. In a 2-quart pan, add the milk over medium heat and cook until just warmed.
3. In another pan, melt the butter and add the flour, stirring continuously.
4. Cook for about 2 minutes. Reduce the heat to low and stir in the milk for about 3-5 minutes. In a large bowl, add the egg yolks and with a fork, beat well.
5. Add a small amount of the milk sauce and stir to combine.
6. Add the remaining milk sauce and beat until well combined.
7. Add the cheese, fresh herbs, mustard, nutmeg, salt and pepper and stir to combine.
8. In another bowl, add the egg whites and beat until soft peaks form.
9. Fold half of the whipped egg whites into the sauce.
10. Gently fold in the remaining whipped egg whites.
11. Transfer the mixture into the prepared soufflé dish.
12. Cook in the oven for about 45 minutes.
13. Remove from the oven and serve immediately.

POTATO
Soufflé

Prep Time: 20 mins
Total Time: 1 hr 20 mins

Servings per Recipe: 4
Calories	180.2
Fat	0.2g
Cholesterol	0.1mg
Sodium	313.6mg
Carbohydrates	40.7g
Protein	4.8g

Ingredients

4 potatoes, peeled and cut into chunks
1 leek, cleaned and sliced
1 1/2 C. hot water
1/2 tsp salt
fresh ground pepper
2 tbsp nonfat milk

Directions

1. In a pan, add the potatoes and enough water to cover and bring to a boil.
2. Reduce the heat and simmer for about 10 minutes.
3. Drain the potatoes, reserving 1/4 C. of the cooking liquid.
4. Heat a medium, greased nonstick skillet over medium-high heat and cook the
5. leek, hot water, salt and pepper until all the liquid is absorbed, stirring occasionally.
6. With a potato masher, mash the potatoes into a bowl.
7. Add the milk and the reserved cooking liquid, one tbsp at a time and mix until fluffy.
8. Stir in the cooked leek.
9. Transfer the mixture into a greased 1-quart soufflé dish and keep aside, covered up to 2 hours.
10. Set your oven to 450 degrees F.
11. Cook, uncovered in the oven for about 30 minutes.

Mac & Cheese Soufflé

Prep Time: 15 mins
Total Time: 1 hr 15 mins

Servings per Recipe: 4
Calories   568.3
Fat   36.6g
Cholesterol   252.0mg
Sodium   678.2mg
Carbohydrates   35.3g
Protein   24.2g

Ingredients

- 3/4 C. dried short cut macaroni
- 6 tbsp butter
- 3 tbsp dried breadcrumbs
- 1 tsp paprika
- 1/3 C. white flour
- 1 1/4 C. milk
- 3/4 C. cheddar cheese, grated
- 2/3 C. freshly grated Parmesan cheese
- 3 eggs, separated
- salt
- pepper

Directions

1. Set your oven to 300 degrees F before doing anything else and arrange a rack in the center of the oven.
2. Grease a 5 C. soufflé dish with a little butter and then, coat the dish with the breadcrumbs, shaking off the excess. In a pan of lightly salted boiling water, cook the macaroni for about 8 minutes.
3. In a pan, melt the butter and stir in the flour and paprika until well combined.
4. Cook for about 1 minute, stirring continuously. Slowly, stir in the milk and cook until mixture becomes thick, stirring continuously.
5. Add the grated cheeses, salt and black pepper and stir until melted completely. Remove from the heat and keep aside to cool slightly. Add the egg yolks and beat until well combined. In a bowl, add the egg whites and beat until soft peaks form.
6. Add 1/4 of the whipped egg whites into the sauce mixture, beating gently to combine.
7. Gently, fold in the remaining egg whites. Then, gently fold in the macaroni.
8. Place the mixture into the prepared soufflé dish.
9. Cook in the oven for about 40-45 minutes.
10. Remove from the oven and serve immediately.

LEMONY
Raspberry Soufflé

🥣 Prep Time: 15 mins
🕐 Total Time: 30 mins

Servings per Recipe: 4
Calories   53.8
Fat   0.0g
Cholesterol   0.0mg
Sodium   54.7mg
Carbohydrates   9.7g
Protein   3.6g

Ingredients

1 1/2 C. raspberry puree
2 tbsp sugar
4 egg whites

1/4 tsp lemon juice
1 tbsp sugar, for ramekins

Directions

1. Set your oven to 400 degrees F before doing anything else and lightly, grease 4 ramekins. Then sprinkle each ramekin with sugar.
2. In a blender, add the raspberry puree and 1 tbsp of the sugar and pulse at medium speed for about 1 minute.
3. Transfer the mixture into a large bowl.
4. In a bowl, add the egg whites, sugar and lemon juice and beat until stiff and fluffy.
5. Gently, fold the egg whites into the raspberry mixture.
6. Divide the mixture into the prepared ramekins evenly.
7. Cook in the oven for about 12-15 minutes.
8. Remove from the oven and serve immediately.

Pepperoni & Cheese Soufflé

Prep Time: 5 mins
Total Time: 35 mins

Servings per Recipe: 6
Calories	558.2
Fat	35.0g
Cholesterol	271.6mg
Sodium	1067.4mg
Carbohydrates	30.0g
Protein	29.1g

Ingredients

- 8 oz. muenster cheese, grated
- 5 eggs
- 1 1/2 C. flour
- 2 C. milk
- 1/2 lb. sliced pepperoni, diced
- 1 tsp oregano
- 1/4 C. grated Parmesan cheese

Directions

1. Set your oven to 425 degrees F before doing anything else and grease a 6-8-quart baking dish.
2. In a bowl, add all the ingredients and mix until well combined.
3. Transfer the mixture into the prepared baking dish.
4. Cook in the oven for about 30 minutes.
5. Remove from the oven and serve immediately.

MILKY
Asparagus Soufflé

🥣 Prep Time: 10 mins
🕐 Total Time: 55 mins

Servings per Recipe: 6
Calories 155.3
Fat 10.6g
Cholesterol 144.9mg
Sodium 419.2mg
Carbohydrates 8.2g
Protein 7.7g

Ingredients

3 tbsp butter, melted
3 tbsp flour
1 C. milk
4 eggs, separated
2 1/2 C. diced asparagus
3/4 tsp salt

Directions

1. Set your oven to 325 degrees F before doing anything else and grease a casserole dish.
2. In a pan, mix together the melted butter and flour.
3. Slowly, add the milk, beating continuously until thickened.
4. Remove from the heat and keep aside.
5. In a bowl, add the egg yolks and beat until thick and lemon colored.
6. Add the asparagus and salt and stir to combine.
7. Add the asparagus mixture into the sauce and stir to combine.
8. In another bowl, add the egg whites and beat until stiff.
9. Gently, fold the whipped egg whites into the asparagus mixture.
10. Place the mixture into the prepared casserole dish.
11. Arrange the casserole dish in a roasting pan with hot water and cook in the oven for about 45 minutes.

Pumpkin Soufflé

Prep Time: 20 mins
Total Time: 1 hr 15 mins

Servings per Recipe: 8
Calories	84.2
Fat	6.0g
Cholesterol	116.9mg
Sodium	112.3mg
Carbohydrates	1.3g
Protein	5.9g

Ingredients

- 8 tiny pumpkins
- 4 large eggs, separated
- 4 tsp all-purpose flour
- 1/4 tsp baking powder
- 3 oz. habanero cheddar cheese
- salt & fresh ground pepper, to taste

Directions

1. Set your oven to 350 degrees F before doing anything else.
2. In a large shallow baking dish, arrange the pumpkins.
3. Add about 1/4-inch of the water.
4. With a piece of the foil, cover the baking dish tightly and cook in the oven for about 40 minutes.
5. Remove from the oven and keep aside to cool.
6. Now, set your oven to 375 degrees F.
7. With a paring knife, remove tops from each pumpkin.
8. Remove the seeds and then, scoop out the flesh, leaving about 1/4-inch-thick shell.
9. In a bowl, add about 4 C. of the pumpkin flesh and keep aside.
10. Add the egg yolks into the bowl of pumpkin flesh and mix well.
11. Add the flour and baking powder and mix well.
12. Add the cheese, salt and pepper and stir to combine.
13. In another bowl, add the egg whites and beat until stiff peaks form.
14. Fold the whipped egg whites into pumpkin mixture.
15. Carefully, place the mixture into the pumpkin shells.
16. Arrange the filled pumpkin shells onto a baking sheet and cook in the oven for about 12-15 minutes.

NUTTY Pecan Soufflé

Prep Time: 10 mins
Total Time: 50 mins

Servings per Recipe: 4
Calories	561.7
Fat	38.6g
Cholesterol	232.5mg
Sodium	356.9mg
Carbohydrates	48.1g
Protein	10.2g

Ingredients

1 loaf cinnamon raisin bread
1 (20 oz.) cans of undrained pineapple
1 C. margarine (melted)
1/2 C. sugar

5 eggs, slightly beaten
1/2 C. chopped pecans

Directions

1. Set your oven to 350 degrees F before doing anything else and grease a 13x9-inch baking dish.
2. Carefully, remove the thin crusts from the bread loaf and then, tear into small pieces.
3. Arrange the bread pieces in the bottom of prepared baking dish and top with the pineapple with the juice evenly.
4. Keep aside.
5. Ina bowl, add the margarine and sugar and beat until creamy.
6. Add the eggs and mix well.
7. Place the egg mixture over bread and pineapple evenly and sprinkle with the pecans.
8. Cook in the oven for about 40 minutes.

Carrot Soufflé

Prep Time: 20 mins
Total Time: 1 hr 5 mins

Servings per Recipe: 10
Calories   284.0
Fat   13.5g
Cholesterol   93.0mg
Sodium   55.3mg
Carbohydrates   37.5g
Protein   4.4g

Ingredients

nonstick cooking spray
5 large eggs, separated
2 C. carrots, finely grated
1 C. sugar
3/4 C. matzo meal
1/2 C. vegetable oil
1 tsp lemon juice
2 tbsp orange juice
1 (20 oz.) cans crushed pineapple in syrup

Directions

1. Set your oven to 350 degrees F before doing anything else and grease a 9x9-inch square baking dish with the cooking spray.
2. In a small bowl, add the egg yolks and beat slightly.
3. In another large bowl, add the egg whites and beat until stiff.
4. Gently, fold in carrots, sugar, and matzo meal.
5. Add the whipped egg yolks, lemon juice, orange juice, oil and pineapple with heavy syrup and gently, stir to combine.
6. Transfer the mixture into the prepared baking dish.
7. Cook in the oven for about 40-45 minutes.

SQUASH & Applesauce Soufflé

Prep Time: 20 mins
Total Time: 35 mins

Servings per Recipe: 4
Calories 133.2
Fat 8.3g
Cholesterol 108.2mg
Sodium 380.8mg
Carbohydrates 11.6g
Protein 4.2g

Ingredients

12 oz. frozen cooked squash
2 tbsp butter
2 tbsp light brown sugar
1/2 tsp salt

1/4 C. unsweetened applesauce
2 eggs, separated
1/8 tsp cream of tartar

Directions

1. Set your oven to 325 degrees F before doing anything else and arrange a rack in the middle of oven.
2. Wrap a greased piece of foil around a greased Soufflé dish.
3. In a pan, add the squash over low heat and cook until heated completely, stirring occasionally.
4. Remove from the heat and add the egg yolks, butter, sugar and salt, beating continuously until well combined.
5. Add the applesauce and gently, stir to combine.
6. Keep aside to cool slightly.
7. In a bowl, add the egg whites and cream of tartar and beat until stiff but not dry.
8. Gently fold the whipped egg whites into the squash mixture.
9. Place the mixture into the prepared Soufflé dish.
10. Cook in the oven for about 35 minutes.
11. Remove from the oven and serve immediately.